AQA Psychology
A Level Paper Three

Relationships

The Extending Knowledge and Skills series is a fresh approach to A Level Psychology, designed for the greater demands of the new AQA specification and assessment, and especially written to stretch and challenge students aiming for higher grades.

Dealing with the topic of AQA's **Paper 3: Relationships**, this book is deliberately laid out with the assessment objectives in mind, from **AO1: Knowledge and understanding** material, followed by **AO2: Application material**, to **AO3: Evaluation and analysis** material. Providing the most in-depth, accessible coverage available of individual topics in Paper 3, the text is packed full of pedagogical features, including:

- **Question time** features to ensure that the reader is consistently challenged throughout the book.
- **New research** sections clearly distinguished within each chapter to ensure readers have access to cutting-edge material.
- A clear focus on the **assessment objectives** for the paper topic to ensure readers know when and where to apply knowledge.
- The use of **example answers with examiner-style comments** to provide greater insight into how to/how not to answer exam questions.

An engaging, relevant and challenging text that broadens student understanding beyond that of the average textbook, this is the essential companion for any student taking the AQA A Level Paper 3 in Psychology.

Phil Gorman is an experienced psychology teacher and Assistant Principal Examiner for Paper 3 of the AQA A Level Psychology specification. He has been teaching this subject at A Level for over 25 years and examining for roughly the same amount of time. His examining experience has, in the past, taken him to the position of Chief Examiner for Edexcel A Level Psychology.

Extending Knowledge and Skills Series

The *Extending Knowledge and Skills Series* is a fresh approach to A Level psychology, designed for greater demands of the new AQA specification and assessment, and especially written to stretch and challenge students aiming for higher grades.

Going beyond the reach of traditional revision textbooks, each book in the series provides wider explanations and greater levels of detail on each of the main topics within each paper option and shows how to apply this knowledge in an exam setting to produce higher tier responses.

Books in the Series:

AQA Psychology A Level Paper Three: Issues and Debates
Phil Gorman

AQA Psychology A Level Paper Three: Relationships
Phil Gorman

AQA Psychology A Level Paper Three: Schizophrenia
Phil Gorman

AQA PSYCHOLOGY A LEVEL PAPER THREE

RELATIONSHIPS

Phil Gorman

Routledge
Taylor & Francis Group

LONDON AND NEW YORK

First published 2020
by Routledge
2 Park Square, Milton Park, Abingdon, Oxon OX14 4RN

and by Routledge
52 Vanderbilt Avenue, New York, NY 10017

Routledge is an imprint of the Taylor & Francis Group, an informa business

© 2020 Phil Gorman

British Library Cataloguing-in-Publication Data
A catalogue record for this book is available from the British Library

Library of Congress Cataloging-in-Publication Data
A catalog record has been requested for this book

ISBN: 978-0-367-40390-4 (hbk)
ISBN: 978-0-367-40391-1 (pbk)
ISBN: 978-0-429-35583-7 (ebk)

Typeset in Goudy Old Style and Frutiger
by Servis Filmsetting Ltd, Stockport, Cheshire

Contents

Illustrations

Figures

Tables

Chapter 1
Introduction

The aims of this book

This book is intended for A Level Psychology students studying the AQA syllabus and has been developed in order to provide further elaboration for the main Paper 3 topics. This particular book will deal with the optional topic of Relationships from section B of Paper 3.

The book has been deliberately laid out with the assessment objectives in mind, so you will find AO1 – Knowledge and Understanding material first, followed by AO2 – Application material, and then AO3 – Evaluation and Analysis material.

Each of the assessment objectives will have an injunction/command word or some other indication that will give you an idea of the particular objective being assessed and how you are supposed to answer the question.

AO1 will include some of the following injunctions/commands words that will indicate you are required to show knowledge and understanding:

Compare – Identify similarities and differences.
Identify – Name or state what it is.
Name – Identify using a technical term.
Describe – Provide an account of.
Distinguish – Explain how two things differ.
Explain – Show what the purpose or reason for something is.
Give – Provide an answer from memory or from the information shown.
Outline – Provide the main characteristics.
State – Clearly set out.
What is meant by – Provide a definition.

AO2 will open with some kind of stem which might be in the form of some information which you will need to refer to in your answer. For example:

Question 1

Is there such a thing as love at first sight and, if there is, what is it that makes us fall in love with someone? Are there certain features that make some people attractive or is it that some people seem like a good match for us?

With reference to the material above, explain physical attractiveness as a factor affecting attraction in romantic relationships?

Alternatively, AO2 questions will provide a description of a scenario with the names of some fictional characters who are involved in a situation that is relevant to an area of psychology. You could then be asked to explain this situation using knowledge derived from the relevant topic. For example:

Question 2

Bill and Ben have been in a relationship for 50 years and every Friday evening Ben buys Bill a bunch of flowers. Ben has never missed a week in 50 years and every Friday Bill gives Ben a big hug in return.

Using the material above, explain how social exchange theory would explain Bill's behaviour. Is there any other explanation for it?

Questions with a stem like this, which then ask you to refer to the stem in some way, are looking to assess AO2 and you have to make sure that you make clear reference to the stem by using some of the information as part of your answer. You will see examples of these in the coming chapters with some sample answers to show you how to deal with them.

AO3 will include one or both of the following injunctions/commands words, indicating that you are required to demonstrate skills of analysis and evaluation:

Discuss – Present strengths and weaknesses of a topic (in 16 mark questions, this can also require some element of description and can be taken as similar to describe and evaluate).

Evaluate – Make a judgement about a topic with reference to evidence.

One of the important features of this book and other books in the series is that there is a clear emphasis on the kinds of skills required for the A Level Psychology exam, so the plenary sections use questions that are focused on exam skills and, at the end of every chapter, there are some exam-style questions with advice on how to answer them and examples of the kinds of answers that could be given to gain very high marks. Key words will be presented in bold and placed in a glossary at the end of each chapter, to make it easier to follow what these words mean and be able to use them more readily yourself.

Further features include an emphasis on new research that is both up to date and challenging, so there will be topics that don't just follow the usual pattern but will make you think again about the kinds of topics that you are studying.

The book also uses the technique of interleaving by bringing back topics from earlier studies to reinforce and consolidate earlier learning. All too often topics that have been studied earlier can be forgotten and it has been shown that by regularly revisiting these topics, it is possible to remember much more easily than by simply trying to cram them all in at the end.

Why are relationships important?

Relationships are important to all of us. They provide us with support and companionship and, in many, cases love and affection. We appear to be driven towards romantic and sexual relationships and the importance of these is highlighted by the amount of time we devote to talking about them, writing books and making films about them, and generally focusing on every detail of our own and other people's love lives. It seems as though there is something of an obsession with them and that maybe we find it very hard to live without them – but we also seem to find it very hard to live *with* them.

> **Question Time**
>
> Why do think there is so much time and space in newspapers, magazines and social media given over to discussing celebrity relationships?
>
> Do you think it has an effect on the kind of relationships that 'real' people have or is it just a form of escape?
>
> What about other forms of the media, e.g. TV and films? Does the portrayal of romantic relationships in those have an effect?

In order to understand the importance of romantic relationships, it might be worth considering the following question.

Which do you think would be worse, the loss of your job or the breakdown of your romantic relationship?

The answer to this question is likely to create a lot of further questions with regard to how long the relationship has been going, what the job is and the level of investment in each. However, it seems as though romantic relationships are at least as

Figure 1.1 Celebrity relationships

important as a person's job and probably slightly more important. After all, if you were to ask someone as they approach the end of their working life if they wished they had spent more time at work or more time with their partner, it's unlikely that they would choose work, unless of course the relationship is quite bad, in which case I'm not sure it counts.

What is covered in the Relationships topic?

The first part of this topic considers the **evolutionary explanations for partner preferences** and whether or not your choice of sexual partner is driven by evolutionary pressures linked to the need to reproduce. Could it be that you are choosing a partner purely because they offer your offspring a better chance of survival? Do men look for a partner who has the best chance of bearing healthy children and do women look for a partner who can best provide for their babies?

However, the main focus of this topic is on romantic relationships and an important part of this relates to the **factors affecting attraction**, including physical attractiveness, proximity and similarity, and how much a person is prepared to reveal about themselves as a relationship develops.

Activity 1

Put the following in order in relation to how important they are to you when considering starting a romantic relationship:

1. Good prospects as a father/mother for your children
2. Openness and honesty
3. Close to where you live
4. Physical attractiveness
5. Similar type of person to you.

There may, of course, be other factors that affect your attraction to another person, but these are the kinds of factors covered in this topic for this specification.

New research

What Leads to Romantic Attraction: Similarity, Reciprocity, Security, or Beauty? Evidence from a Speed-Dating Study

Shanhong Luo and Guangjian Zhang. University of North Carolina at Wilmington, University of Notre Dame

First published: 1 July 2009

In this research, the authors have chosen to look at four factors affecting attraction: sharing similar characteristics; having attraction reciprocated; physical attractiveness; ability to maintain a close and secure relationship. These are all factors that have been studied many times by a variety of researchers but have mostly been conducted in lab-based experiments with artificially created scenarios that only lead to hypothetical conclusions based on how someone 'might' react.

This research was designed to examine initial attraction in a real-life setting with people actually searching for a partner who are likely to provide an honest picture of the reasons for their choices – speed dating. The authors wanted to make the research setting as realistic as possible, so they recreated a speed dating session in a classroom at their university and recruited 108 single, heterosexual students aged between 17 and 26, who took part in exchange for course credits.

The four factors outlined above were examined with a series of questionnaires to establish their physical, demographic and personality characteristics, as well as their social and leisure interests. Having established certain features of each participant prior to the speed dating session, it was possible to correlate these with questions about how attractive they were to members of the opposite sex obtained both during and after the sessions.

Their findings were unsurprising in one way, i.e. the most consistent factor related to attraction was physical attractiveness for both men and women. However, they were slightly surprising in another way, i.e. similarity of characteristics was not a significant factor in attraction, whether or not attraction was reciprocated made no difference (although within the context of a five-minute date it was difficult to measure this), and women were less concerned about their partner's secure attachment characteristics than men. Women only seemed to be interested in the man's level of physical attractiveness and sporting interests, whereas men's attraction to women was related to a range of characteristics, including agreeableness, conscientiousness, low levels of anxiety and age (men seemed to prefer slightly older women).

The conclusion of this seems to be that physical attractiveness is really important (when you only have five minutes to judge someone!), hardly a surprising result. But also that women are somewhat shallower than men and that men seem to be searching for a somewhat more stable partner.

Question time

Do you find the results of this research surprising? If so, in what way?

What do you think of the methodology employed in this research? Is it realistic?

Theories of romantic relationships

Once you have decided that you are attracted to someone and maybe started dating them, psychologists want to understand how these relationships develop and are maintained, and also why they might break down as they may well do (please excuse the cynicism).

Activity 2

Ernie and Bert have been in a relationship for 50 years and are very happy together. On Wednesdays Ernie goes to chess club where he meets a few friends, on Thursdays Bert plays bowls at his local club and every Friday night they have date night. At home, Ernie does all the housework and Bert does all the DIY. They both work and although Bert earns quite a lot more money than Ernie, it's Ernie who sorts out all the financial matters. The house they own is in both their names and they recently made wills to make sure that the other one was provided for in the event of their death. In 50 years, they have never forgotten to get each other an anniversary card to celebrate the beginning of their relationship and each year the cards have a picture of a rubber duck on them, which is a symbol of their devotion to each other.

Consider the (fictional) example of the relationship above. Read through the material and try to identify as many points as you can that show why Ernie and Bert have such a successful relationship. Once you have done this, make a note of any other factors that you believe contribute to a successful romantic relationship.

You probably came up with some of the points below:

Costs and benefits	The benefits of the relationship are higher than the costs.
Equal division of labour	There is a fairly equal division of tasks and it seems that even though they may not do the same things, the way that things are divided up is fair.
Commitment	Both of them have given over a lot of time and commitment to the relationship, which provides a high degree of satisfaction for both.

Undoubtedly, some of these factors are important in the development and maintenance of romantic relationships and the absence of some of them is likely to provide an explanation for the breakdown of relationships. However, they are unlikely to be the only reasons and there are bound to be many other factors that make for a successful relationship.

New forms of relationships

The introduction of the internet and the growth of social media have changed the kinds of relationships we have. In the past we may have only had a few friends, people that we knew from our local area, school, pub or any other places we frequented regularly. We may have had a penfriend, who would be someone that we communicated with regularly but who lived too far away for us to see regularly, and who might actually live in a foreign country though still with the likelihood that we would have met them at some time, e.g. on a holiday to another country, or to another town a long way from home.

One area of research in this topic concerns **virtual relationships in social media** and how we are now able to form both friendships and romantic relationships online through the internet and maintain them through social media. This has a number of advantages and disadvantages when compared to face-to-face relationships.

Activity 3

Try to think of as many advantages and disadvantages as you can for virtual relationships that are formed and maintained through the internet and social media (the first one on each side has been done for you).

Advantages	Disadvantages
Able to come into contact with people a long way from home who you would otherwise never have the chance to meet.	As you are sometimes unable to see the person, you can't be sure that they are telling the truth about themselves.

It seems that there are a number of advantages and disadvantages for each type and although it is true that many more young people are establishing these forms of relationships, it is also quite common for somewhat older people to make use of them, even if this is in a way that is one or two steps behind the younger generation. I was recently informed by one of my students that they weren't surprised that I was using Facebook as it's really for older people!

The final kind of relationship covered in this topic isn't actually all that new but is certainly regarded as a current phenomenon – even though the actual term '**parasocial relationship**' was first defined more than 50 years ago.

This form of relationship is most usually associated with the kind of celebrity adoration that has been going for a very long time now. It involves people feeling as though they know and are sometimes actually in love with someone, when the person they are adoring or in love with has no idea that they exist. Although this is most associated with celebrities, it could also apply to organisations such as football teams or even products or brands that people become obsessed with, e.g. The Marmite Appreciation Society.

As stated above, this form of relationship has existed for some time. Back in my childhood, I recall my sister being obsessed with David Cassidy (OK, I know you've never heard of him, but trust me he was big back in the day). Often these kinds of relationships can be harmless and cause no problems at all as fans just really like that person for their music or entertainment value, but they can also become pathological when fans become really obsessed and believe that they have an actual relationship with that person. This might lead to stalking or other forms of obsessive behaviour that end up being dangerous for all concerned.

New research

BBC

Newsbeat

2 June 2017

Stan, from the Eminem song of the same name, is now an official word in the *Oxford English Dictionary* (*OED*).

The track, from Eminem's *The Marshall Mathers*, features Dido. It is about a crazed fan obsessed with the rapper.

The **dictionary entry says a 'stan' is 'an overzealous or obsessive fan of a particular celebrity'.**

It also gives a helpful example about how it might be used. 'He has millions of stans who are obsessed with him and call him a rap god.'

The lyrics to the original song tell the story of how a fan gets increasingly upset that Eminem isn't writing back to him. The rapper finally realises that Stan has become so desperate that he has killed himself and his pregnant girlfriend. The *OED* says the word stan can be used as both a noun and a verb.

Question time

What does this article tell us about the rise of parasocial relationships?

Do you think that it's right that this word has been included in the *OED*?

Should this be regarded as a 'big' problem?

Summary

This introduction should have got you ready for more of this kind of discussion and will hopefully aid you in your further understanding of these fascinating topics.

Chapter 2
Sexual selection and human reproductive behaviour

Spec check

The evolutionary explanations for partner preferences, including the relationship between sexual selection and human reproductive behaviour

AO1 (Knowledge and understanding): Sexual selection and human reproductive behaviour

From an evolutionary point of view, species survive because they are able to adapt to their changing environmental conditions and this adaptation leads to beings that are better suited to their environment. It would be surprising therefore, if we didn't assume that evolution has something to do with the way in which we procreate and make choices about whom we do and do not procreate with.

In *The Descent of Man* (1981 [1871]), Darwin discusses the issue of sexual selection and the way that certain features of species are not merely related to natural selection and therefore their ability to survive but also to increase their chances of obtaining a mate. The distinction is made between primary sexual characteristics, such as gonads, which distinguish males from females and are directly related to procreation, and secondary sexual characteristics, such as greater height, which distinguish one human from another and may provide an advantage in attracting a mate or in battling against other humans for a potential mate.

In order to understand how sexual selection affects males and females differently, it is necessary to consider the concept of sexual dimorphism, which relates to the different characteristics possessed by males and females and how these characteristics increase their chances of survival and procreation.

An important part of the difference in the characteristics of males and females relates to anisogamy, which is the difference between the nature and number of male and female sex cells (gametes). Male gametes (sperm) are very small, highly mobile and constantly being produced in large numbers; the average male will produce over 500 billion sperm cells in a lifetime (shedding around 1 billion per month) and a healthy adult male can release around 200 million sperm cells in one ejaculation and each sperm cell has the potential to fertilise an egg, so each ejaculation has the potential to produce 200 million babies! Female gametes (eggs) on the other hand are much larger, immobile and produced in quite small numbers for a relatively short time period. Although women are born with 2 million egg follicles, most of these close up by puberty and an average healthy female will release 300–450 eggs in a lifetime, usually 1 for every month between puberty and the menopause.

Question time

In evolutionary terms, what effect will these differences on the sexual activity of males and females?

Will it affect their choice of mate differently?

In order to ensure the survival of their genes, what should men do? What should women do?

Intrasexual selection

This refers to the strategies that are adopted within each sex and therefore looks at the way that members of the same sex compete in order to obtain a mate. This is mainly focused upon the males as, due to the points made above about anisogamy, there will be many men competing to get access to the most fertile females who, in turn, will be holding out for the best possible male specimen.

One strategy employed by males is mate-guarding, which involves trying to keep away other males who will inevitably want to mate with a fertile female. Males know this all too well as it is something that they would like to do, and it is therefore quite realistic to suspect other males of wanting to do the same. They also fear that they may expend a lot of resources on their female partner only for her to go and get pregnant by someone else. After all, the rise of the paternity test offered by TV programmes like Jeremy Kyle shows that males can never be sure (without a DNA test) that they are the father of their partner's child. Unfortunately, this strategy is time- and resource-consuming so the simpler strategy may just be to attempt to procreate with as many fertile females as possible, particularly if you can get some other male to bring them up for you!

The law of battle is a term used to describe how male animals compete for the right to procreate with the females and this is often the main strategy employed by males, such that the strongest, fittest and best endowed (with large muscles, for instance) are likely to succeed and earn their right. This helps to explain the dimorphism found in the male and female physical form: males have an evolutionary advantage by being taller and stronger, whereas females have no evolutionary advantage from having these characteristics, therefore they are likely to be passed down in males but not in females.

However, if male competition were enough to explain how sexual selection occurs then this section would be very short as we would simply say that the stronger and fitter you are then the greater your chance of reproductive success. Female choice would play no part in it because mate choice would simply be decided by the winner of the battle.

Unfortunately, or fortunately depending on your point of view, size or strength, this isn't enough and Darwin recognised this and devoted a lot of pages to explaining why and how an equally or even more important factor in mate choice was that employed by the female. After all, she is the one who is in a better position to be choosy.

Intersexual selection

This refers to the strategies that are adopted between the sexes and therefore looks at the way that males and females attempt to attract and choose partners. This is often focused on the female as it is believed she will be the choosier due to the factors outlined above. If the female needs to find a suitable mate for her precious eggs, then she is likely to choose and seek to attract the best available mate. The position of the female is strengthened by the fact that fertility amongst women is limited (due to anisogamy) and as such, while there may be many fertile males, there are far fewer fertile females and so the female can afford to be choosy. Also, the consequences of making a bad choice are significantly worse for the female as she will have spent many months carrying the baby and many more bringing it up, so this precious time should not be wasted on raising a child that is unlikely to survive or at least survive long enough and well enough to procreate.

Females will adopt certain strategies to ensure the best possible genes and best possible father for their offspring:

- 'Sexy sons' hypothesis – females will seek mates with the most attractive features as these features are more likely to be passed on to their male offspring who will, in turn, have a better chance of mating (Fisher, 1999; first published in 1930).
- Courting rituals – females will encourage males to engage in long and elaborate displays to encourage them to commit to the relationship and hopefully therefore to their child.

Question time

What do you think? Are there clear differences between the strategies employed by males and females?

Is it right to say that females are choosy, and males aren't?

Mini plenary

Write a paragraph to explain the difference between intrasexual selection and intersexual selection.

AO2 (Application of knowledge): How does the issue apply in practice?

The holism and reductionism debate

According to holism, we cannot understand the nature of something unless we take into account the social, mental and economic factors as well as the physical, chemical and biological factors. The whole is therefore greater than the sum of its parts and as such to simply try to focus on any one of the factors above would be pointless.

Reductionism, on the other hand, tries to look at single factors that influence something, and it is parsimonious as it believes that the simplest explanation is often the best. For example, in the context of evolution, we could simply focus on the biological factors that influence development and argue that it is they that should be focused on to explain behaviour.

Interleave me now

Sexual selection and the holism–reductionism debate

Sexual selection is regarded as a natural process and as such it is influenced by the inheritance of genetic structures that cause us to behave in certain ways. The concept of sexual selection is therefore one that attempts to reduce human behaviour to biological structures and could be regarded as biologically reductionist. Darwin was keen to do this in order to gain acceptance from the scientific community, thus showing that his work was not merely philosophical and based on conjecture but based on scientific evidence and fact. This focuses sexual selection on a process that will have necessarily evolved over an extremely long period.

The alternative to reductionism is holism and this attempts to place behaviour in the context of all the possible influences that *may* be involved and as such provides a fuller but less focused explanation, which offers up potential influences rather than specific evidential ones. In the case of sexual selection, it would be possible (using a holistic account) to speculate on a range of factors that influence males and females in their choice of mate of which evolutionary pressures would be just one.

The focus on higher levels of explanation would push us towards a consideration of psychological, social and cultural influences on the choice of mating partner.

Think!

What kind of psychological, social and cultural factors might influence our choice of mate?

Why might these factors be more important to humans than to other species?

Are all of these consistent with an evolutionary view in which we choose a mate in order to ensure the survival of our genes and offspring?

Psychological factors that could come into play might include a tendency towards finding someone who matches us in some ways, e.g. similar physical or personality characteristics that might help us to get along and stay together, rather than simply be useful to us in producing healthy, long-lasting offspring.

Social factors might include a tendency towards finding someone of a desirable social status and level of wealth who can provide us with a certain standard of living that we find desirable.

Cultural factors might include some consideration of what constitutes beauty or desirability. Between different societies, this is likely to vary from one culture to another, e.g. whether someone would be more desirable if they were tall or short, fat or thin, etc.

Can you think of other examples of social, psychological or cultural factors that influence mate choice?

Psychological	Social	Cultural

AO3 (Analysis and evaluation of knowledge): How useful is this explanation?

Is there evidence to support anisogamy?

Anisogamy would suggest that males would focus on youth and fertility in their mate preference and that females would focus on resources and security in their mate choice. There has been a mass of research since the 1970s looking into this question. For example, in a very large-scale study across a range of countries Buss (1989) showed support for the existence of these preferences.

In more recent times, Gustavsson et al. (2008) provided mixed support from a statistical analysis of online dating websites and personal adverts in Swedish newspapers. They found some support in that males showed a significant preference for younger females, while women showed a slight preference for older males. Also, in line with the theory, many more males offered resources as an inducement than did females. However, they also found that older women were interested in younger men, which doesn't particularly support the theory, although these women were aged between 40 and 79 and therefore not highly fertile.

Most research in this area seems to suggest support for the notion of anisogamy and its role in sexual selection as it seems that (for the most part) youth and fertility are an important consideration for males whereas resources and security are highly valued by females, unless they have gone beyond child-bearing age in which case life expectancy and health may be more important than wealth and security.

How do social and cultural factors challenge the idea of sexual selection?

Reductionism may bring some benefits for the principle of sexual selection as it allows the possibility of isolating one variable to show cause and effect. However, it also ignores a range of other possible influences and it is likely that the changing social and cultural circumstances in which we find ourselves will have an effect on people's behaviour – and this is particularly true in relation to the changing social roles of men and women.

Even if we accept that a woman's role was once confined to the question of finding a good father for her child, then it's likely that this was (at least in part) influenced by her position in society and the fact that women had fewer rights and freedoms, rather than due to evolutionary pressures. This can be seen most dramatically now that the rights and freedoms of women have changed, at least in British society, where women are now in a better position to make choices based on other factors as they are able to have a career and are not dependent on men to provide resources.

Furthermore, this changing position means that women can make a choice whether to have children or not, and they may decide to try to find a mate who has similar preferences, it is likely that there are other men out there who are also not subject to the evolutionary pressure of passing on their genes. Methods of contraception mean that women are still able to have as much sex as they want without the risk of pregnancy and the responsibilities that go with that. This changing position would also make it easier for homosexual women to follow their true sexuality in an environment that is less reliant on having a male partner as a provider.

Is it possible to compare humans to animals?

The question of the ability to compare humans to animals is always one that is raised when looking at evolutionary issues. Even though Darwin devoted considerable time to discussing human sexual selection in *The Descent of Man*, the issue of being able to compare evidence from very simple organisms to very complex humans is always raised.

A couple of issues are raised by Wilson et al. (2017): the first is that humans are large, grow and reproduce slowly and live in large complex societies; secondly, humans have unique qualities not possessed by other species, e.g. language and abstract reasoning. This clearly poses many problems when attempting to compare humans with other, less complex, species.

However, Wilson et al. also offered the alternative argument that the variability in human behaviour has provided many opportunities to further investigate and develop sexual selection theory further. Darwin believed that sexual selection was the driving force behind the variation in the characteristics of humans and also in the differences between men and women. Over a long period of time, we have seen not only rapid evolution in biological characteristics but also in cultural characteristics.

Consequently, Wilson et al. see many challenges being offered by comparing humans with other species, but they also see many opportunities and go further to argue that it is impossible to study humans in isolation from other species and that only by comparing humans to other primates can we make sense of the Darwinian theory of sexual selection.

Is intrasexual selection restricted to men?

According to the theory laid out so far, intersexual selection will be favoured by women and intrasexual selection by men. However, it's possible that intrasexual selection may also be useful to women in certain circumstances, although it is a risky strategy and can have the opposite effect of driving potential mates away.

Arnocky (2016) has argued that physical violence is unlikely to be used by females in their battles with other females to attract a mate (unlike their male counterparts) as they have too much to lose, given that it is they that will be required to do most of the parenting. However, females do use other, verbally aggressive methods to put down their female rivals in the eyes of potential mates in relation to three areas:

1. They will derogate their rival's level of attractiveness
2. They will suggest a level of promiscuity by their rival
3. They will derogate their rival's personality.

These verbal derogations are particularly effective when proposed by more attractive, rather than less attractive, women; and they are more common in situations where the rivalry is more intense (fewer eligible males) and when the women are ovulating, suggesting that verbal derogations are linked to fertility and the desire to procreate with a male. However, Arnocky also found that the strategy had risks attached as it could have the opposite effect and put off a prospective mate who may find such verbal aggression unattractive. The lesson from this seems to be that female rivalry may work to an extent but sometimes even men aren't completely shallow and can recognise inner malice even if they can't always recognise inner beauty.

Mini plenary

Look at the evidence for and against sexual selection and plan out both sides of the argument, following the structure indicated below. Write a short piece of no more than 200 words explaining the case for and against sexual selection.

PLAN

Arguments for:

Arguments against:

Your response:

A modern issue – dating websites and social media

Making friends has changed forever! We can now have many 'friends' that we never meet face-to-face but merely interact with through social media. Similarly, dating isn't done in the same way any more, and wandering down to your local pub or club is no longer the most obvious way to meet a potential partner. The internet has it all there waiting for you with pics and profiles set up for you to sort through and chose the one for you. But even this is changing, or 'evolving' you might say, as social media create ever new ways for us to assess a potential mate.

New research

The evolution of the online dating experience

Getting into the nitty-gritty of online dating reveals a complex user experience evolving toward the ubiquity of social networking

By Jayse Lee

Article No: 1031 | 5 June 2013 |

These days it's not so much a question of whether or not to use dating websites, but how. The sites are now so commonplace that people who would previously never have dreamed of using them are involved and it is open to debate how they should be used.

The profile debate

Profiles have always been an important aspect of the online dating experience, so much so that the way that people browse through them has given rise to a new phrase, 'relationshopping', which explains how users flick through each profile till they find the one they want. However, it isn't always easy to get into a profile the really important things about you, like your sense of humour or dazzling personality.

Emerging trends

The problem is that these websites aren't moving with the times and are still operating on a system that was developed before the ubiquity of the internet was a real phenomenon. These days, the model isn't so much browse, meet, fall in love and then close the account as browse, browse, meet, browse, meet, browse, browse, meet, repeat.

The future of online dating

The future will be no more online dating as the social media sites we already use become integrated into this process and dating changes from something that was done though dating sites to something that is done all the time, subtly and naturally, so that we hardly notice the change.

Question time

What does this tell us about finding a mate in the digital age?

Does this fit with sexual selection?

Is the evolution mentioned in the title of the article the same as the evolution discussed in this chapter? Does it involve adapting to the environment? Is it about survival?

Chapter plenary

1. What is meant by the term sexual selection?
2. What is meant by the term anisogamy?
3. What is the difference between intersexual selection and intrasexual selection?
4. What strategies are used by males to obtain a mate?
5. What strategies are used by females to obtain a mate?
6. What does Darwin mean by natural selection?
7. How do behavioural traits evolve? Give an example.
8. What is the holism–reductionism debate?
9. How is the concept of sexual selection reductionist?
10. What factors would need to be considered to make mate choice/preference holistic? Give examples.
11. What evidence is there to support anisogamy?
12. How do social/cultural factors challenge the idea of sexual selection?
13. Is it possible to compare animals to humans?
14. Is intrasexual selection restricted to men?
15. How does online dating show how mate choice is evolving?

Glossary

Key word	Definition
Anisogamy	Reproduction involving a union of gametes that vary in size and form.
Courtship rituals	Elaborate displays of behaviour usually shown by males in order to convince a female to mate with them.
Egg follicles	Fluid-filled sacs that contain immature eggs.
Evolution	The process by which different kinds of life developed from earlier forms through natural selection.
Gametes	The reproductive cells of males (sperm) and females (ovum).
Holism	The most complex explanation that tries to look at the complete picture to explain behaviour and explore all of the factors that might influence it.
Law of battle	A term used by Darwin to describe competition between males for access to females.
Levels of explanation	The different ways of explaining behaviour organised into a hierarchy based on the depth of their explanation.
Mate-guarding	Behaviour designed to prevent a mate from having intercourse with someone else.
Natural selection	The process by which species change over time through adaptation to their environment.
Primary sexual characteristics	The features of an individual's body directly involved in reproduction that distinguish it from members of the opposite sex, e.g. genitals.
Procreate	The activity of conceiving and bearing offspring (to reproduce).
Reductionism	The simplest explanation that seeks to find a single cause for examples of behaviour.
Secondary sexual characteristics	The features of an individual's body that distinguish it from members of the opposite sex but are not directly involved in reproduction, e.g. height.
Sexual dimorphism	The different characteristics of males and females of the same species other than the sexual organs.
Sexual selection	An evolutionary explanation for how members of one biological sex choose a mate and how members of the same biological sex compete for mates. Characteristics that increase success in these areas are naturally selected.

Key word	Definition
'Sexy sons' hypothesis	The belief that females will choose attractive features in their mate so that those features will be passed on to their male offspring, who will then have a better chance of mating.
Ubiquity	Being very widespread and seeming to be everywhere.

Plenary: Exam-style questions and answers with advisory comments

Question 1.

Explain what is meant by the term sexual selection in psychology? [2 marks]

Marks for this question: AO1 = 2

Advice: In a question like this, it's important to make sure you are making it clear how this relates to psychology, so this will probably require an example. There is no need to provide any analysis or evaluation as both marks are for AO1: Knowledge and understanding.

Possible answer: Sexual selection is an evolutionary explanation for how members of one biological sex choose a mate and how members of the same biological sex compete for mates. Characteristics that increase success in these areas are naturally selected, e.g. greater height in males.

Question 2.

Diane and Pete have decided to have a go at online dating. Diane has created a list of things she is looking for in a man. She feels that it's important that he should have a good job, be at least six feet tall and have all his own teeth! Pete believes that his ideal woman should be between 20 and 35, have a strong sense of loyalty and enjoy cosy nights at home in front of the TV.

With reference to the section above, explain what this tells us about evolutionary explanations for partner preference. [4 marks]

Marks for this question: AO2 = 4

Advice: In this question, it's really important to recognise that all marks are for AO2, which means that you have to show the skill of application to the stem. You will still need to show an understanding of how evolution can explain partner preferences, but this time by picking out the references from the information you have been given. There is still no need to analyse or evaluate.

Possible answer: *Evolutionary explanations focus on the different strategies used by males and females in mate preference. Intersexual selection refers to mate preference strategies, used mainly by females, which focus on obtaining a mate who will help to produce and provide for healthy offspring. Diane is therefore* focusing on the importance of her ideal mate being tall and having good teeth as a sign of good genes, and having a good job shows the ability to provide for any potential children.

Intrasexual selection refers to strategies used mainly by males that focus on ensuring that they have access to a fertile female without fear of competition from other males. Pete is therefore identifying that his ideal woman is young and fertile but also that her loyalty and desire to stay at home a lot would make her less likely to attract or show an interest in other men.

Question 3.

Discuss the relationship between sexual selection and human reproductive behaviour.   [16 marks]

Marks for this question: AO1 = 6 and AO3 = 10

Advice: This question is looking for both skills of knowledge and understanding and analysis and evaluation. As there are 6 marks for AO1 and 10 for AO3, there should be greater emphasis on the evaluation. However, all such extended writing questions are marked holistically and therefore it is important that the knowledge is accurate and detailed and that the evaluation is clear and effective.

Possible answer: Sexual selection looks at the way certain characteristics are favoured by members of each sex as they help to obtain a mate and ensure the production of healthy offspring. This leads to the use of different strategies by males and females to ensure they are able to pass on their genes successfully.

Males and females have different strategies due to anisogamy, which is the natural differences in the sex cells (gametes) of males and females. Males have gametes (sperm), which are small, highly mobile and produced regularly in large quantities (usually around 1 billion a month). Consequently, males can spread them around freely and mate with as many females as possible as they can afford to waste some in the hope that some will produce offspring. Females have gametes (ovum), which are large, immobile and produced irregularly in relatively small quantities (usually around one a month). Consequently, females can't afford to waste any and must try to ensure that only the best possible sperm with the best possible genes are able to fertilise her eggs.

Intrasexual selection focuses on strategies used mainly by males to ensure that they alone have access to fertile females. The issue here is about characteristics and behaviour that will improve their chances of competing with other males so that they can ensure their genes are successfully passed on. One strategy used by males is mate-guarding, which involves males trying to prevent other males from gaining access to their mate and trying to prevent their mate from having opportunities to mate with other males. Males will also compete with other males to gain access to fertile females using the law of battle to 'win' their right to mate. Sexual selection tends to favour the production of larger, stronger males.

Intersexual selection focuses on strategies used mainly by females to ensure access to the 'fittest' males who will be able to provide for their offspring after birth. One approach is referred to as the 'sexy sons' hypothesis as it suggests that females will look for the most attractive male features in the hope that these will be passed on to their male offspring who will then have the best mating opportunities themselves. Another important factor for females is to have a mate who will be able to provide for their child so they will encourage potential mates to engage in elaborate courting rituals to show their commitment, e.g. buying dinner or bringing flowers.

As an explanation for human reproductive behaviour, this approach is quite dated, as it doesn't take account of the changing social and cultural factors that influence men and particularly women today.

The position of women in society has changed so much that it's hard to say that women need men for resources, or indeed that women are not engaged in intrasexual selection. It is possible that the desire for a man with resources was due to the fact that women didn't have easy access to those resources in the past and now that they do, they don't need to get that from a man.

Arnocky has also pointed out that women are more than capable of engaging in intrasexual selection, just not necessarily of the physical kind, as they use verbal derogation to put down their rivals. Arnocky suggests that women will question their rival's attractiveness and likely promiscuity in order to give them an advantage.

All of this shows that the kind of sexual selection referred to in this theory may not closely relate to life in the twenty-first century.

A further problem arises with the notion of reductionism as the theory focuses solely on the desire to pass on your genes successfully.

Darwin was keen to produce evidence for this in order to show that his theory was scientific and would therefore gain credibility in the scientific community. Unfortunately, this focus was at the expense of any other factors that might influence someone's behaviour in this regard. There are likely to be social, psychological and cultural factors that come into play, such as finding someone you are likely to be compatible with and you share the same interests with, as these will mean you are more likely to stay together.

While this simple level of explanation is useful as it makes it easier to isolate and study a specific variable, it is probably too simplistic for something as complex as human relationships.

This problem can, in some ways, be traced back to the fact that much of this research is based on animal behaviour, which creates a problem when trying to generalise to human behaviour.

Wilson et al. have argued that the fact that humans live in large, complex societies and are able to use language and abstract reasoning makes them somewhat unique in the animal world and therefore it is also quite hard to generalise animal behaviour to human behaviour.

However, they also argue that the variability in human behaviour shows a high degree of evolution, providing significant opportunities to study this phenomenon, and also that it is impossible to study humans in isolation from other species and therefore a degree of comparison is necessary for a full understanding.

There is certainly plenty of evidence from human behaviour for the influence of sexual selection, particularly when looking at the kinds of characteristics that males and females say they are looking for. In line with the theory, Buss found differences between male and female mate preferences in a large-scale study across 37 countries.

More recently, Gustavsson et al. found mixed support in the dating websites and personal ads they studied, as men did show a tendency to favour younger women and women tended to favour resources, but they also found that women tended to favour older men, although this was only true of women in the older age bracket who were likely to be past their fertile age.

Overall, the evidence from what people say, or, at least, put on dating websites, is supportive of the theory. However, dating is itself evolving so fast that it is hard to know what preferences are being shown, as both males and females use social networking to both connect and create mating opportunities. The future of sexual selection and reproduction is likely to be far too complex to explain through the nature and number of sex cells and is more likely to relate to the ability to navigate successfully through the minefield of social media.

References

Arnocky, S. (2016) Intrasexual rivalry among women. In: V. Weekes-Shackelford and T. Shackelford (eds), *Encyclopedia of Evolutionary Psychological Science*. Cham, Switzerland: Springer.

Buss, D. (1989) Sex differences in human mate preferences: Evolutionary hypotheses tested in 37 cultures. *Behavioral and Brain Sciences*, 12 (1): 1–14.

Darwin, C., (1981 [1871]) *The Descent of Man, and Selection in Relation to Sex*. Princeton, NJ: Princeton University Press.

Fisher, R.A. (1999) *The Genetical Theory of Natural Selection: A Complete Variorum Edition*. Oxford: Oxford University Press.

Gustavsson, L., Johnsson, J.I. and Uller, T. (2008) Mixed support for sexual selection theories of mate preferences in the Swedish population. *Evolutionary Psychology*, 6 (4): 575–585.

Lee, J. (2013) The evolution of the online dating experience. Article No. 1031. 5 June 2013. https://uxmag.com/articles/the-evolution-of-the-online-dating-experience (accessed 12 August 2019).

Wilson, M.L., Miller, C.M. and Crouse, K.N. (2017) Humans as a model species for sexual selection research. *proceedings. Biological Sciences*, 284 (1866), 20171320.

Chapter 3
Factors affecting romantic relationships 1: Self-disclosure

Spec check

Factors affecting attraction in romantic relationships: self-disclosure

AO1 (Knowledge and understanding): Factors affecting romantic relationships: Self-disclosure

Whenever you start seeing someone, the first questions you're asked concern what the other person is like and you can only answer this question if the other person has told you. Self-disclosure involves revealing personal information about yourself to an intimate partner, and it has been suggested that it should be something we are all looking to do as it will hopefully bring us closer to the person that we are starting a relationship with.

However, it's difficult to judge just how much you should reveal and at what point of the relationship, and whether this will have a positive or negative effect.

> **Think!**
>
> What should you disclose on the first date? What if the other person asks you something you didn't want to reveal on a first date?
>
> Is it dishonest not to reveal everything about yourself?

Social penetration theory

According to Altman and Taylor (1973) self-disclosure in a relationship is similar to peeling back the layers of an onion. There is a breadth vs depth issue here as the outer layers are larger and provide greater breadth of information about a person, such as information about their work, education, family background, hobbies and interests. The inner layers are much smaller and are found deeper within the onion and so provide greater depth of information, such as information about their past relationships, hopes and fears, and maybe a few interesting secrets. The outer layers are more superficial and are the sort of thing we would be prepared to reveal to acquaintances, with each layer comes a deeper level of intimacy until we get to the core, which contains information about our true self. This is something that is only likely to be revealed to those we are closest to, if it's ever revealed at all and it's possible that we always hold something back.

Rewards and costs of self-disclosure

Altman and Taylor (1973) suggest that when deciding how much information to disclose we first consider the rewards and costs of doing so. Self-disclosure can clearly bring rewards: as we open up to someone, we draw them closer and gain higher levels of intimacy, which will hopefully be reciprocated. However, revealing private thoughts and feelings can also make us vulnerable and bring embarrassment or a lack of trust if it doesn't lead to the other person also disclosing, so reciprocity is also important. Consequently, deciding how much information to reveal will depend on our assessment of the situation and the person we are revealing to. If we are unsure of how they're going to react then it's likely that we will hold back. This level of certainty is only likely to come from having got to know someone over a significant period of time and through a process of trial and error, so it fits well with Altman and Taylor's view that there are stages of self-disclosure (ranging from the most superficial sharing of information, through increasing levels of openness to the most intimate sharing) that penetrate more deeply as we get to trust someone more. If a relationship has developed in this way further self-disclosure will lead to further intimacy, and if that self-disclosure stops, trust will start to be lost and each person will start to hold back more – potentially leading to the end of the relationship.

Question time

What does social penetration theory tell us about the importance of self-disclosure in relationships?

How would someone feel if their disclosures were not reciprocated?

Is it always a good idea to disclose everything in your most intimate relationship?

Whether or not self-disclosure is seen as attractive is likely to be mediated by factors related to what is being disclosed and who is disclosing it.

Factors affecting self-disclosure

Whether or not self-disclosure is seen as a positive and therefore attractive feature is likely to be influenced by what is being disclosed and who is disclosing it. Collins and Miller (1994) identified four factors that have been shown to influence the attractiveness of self-disclosure.

1. **The appropriateness of the disclosure** – the rule here seems to be that too much too soon is bad – breaking the norms of what might be regarded as appropriate early in the relationship will bring a negative result.
2. **Gender differences** – females are stereotypically seen as better communicators than males and as such it might be more acceptable for females to disclose more. However, social norms may also mean that females are more receptive to personal information and therefore males disclosing personal information to a female may be highly regarded, and for similar reasons males may be less receptive.
3. **Attributions for the disclosure** – this refers to the reasons that we believe someone has disclosed the information to us. If we believe that we have been personally selected to receive this information, then it is deemed to be attractive; but not if we believe that it could have been told to anyone or if it is seen to only be relevant to the situation.
4. **Content of the disclosure** – intimacy is a feature of positive relationships and therefore disclosures that are too impersonal and have low intimacy tend not to be attractive. However, highly personal disclosures can also cause problems as they may make the recipient feel uncomfortable and that they should reciprocate with an equally personal disclosure that may put someone off.

Question time

Do you agree/disagree with the factors identified above?

Can you think of any other factors that have been missed from this list?

Mini plenary

Place the following terms under the correct heading of either social penetration theory or further influences on self-disclosure:

Breadth vs Depth, Gender, Attributions, Rewards vs Costs, Stages of self-disclosure, Content, Appropriateness, Reciprocity.

Social penetration theory	Further influences on self-disclosure

AO2 (Application of knowledge): How does this apply in practice?

Self-disclosure and humanistic psychology

One of the pioneers of research into self-disclosure was Sidney Jourard who believed that self-disclosure was both a sign and a cause of a healthy personality. His research (Jourard, S. 1959) was one of the first to show the relationship between self-disclosure and liking, and he became a leading figure in humanistic psychology. He believed that the path to obtaining self-disclosure in others was to be prepared to disclose yourself and as such argued that psychotherapists should practice openness with their patients in a similar way to Carl Rogers' **client-centred therapy**.

Interleave me now

Rogers' client-centred therapy

In *A Way of Being*, written in the early 1980s, Rogers (1995) explained how the practice of client-centred therapy should be carried out.

The first element is what he refers to as congruence, but he suggests that it could just as easily be referred to as genuineness as he argues that the therapist must be him/herself in the session and not put up a front or any kind of barrier that would prevent the client from disclosing information.

The second element is unconditional positive regard, which involves acceptance and support for the client regardless of what they say or do. This positive attitude will also allow the client to 'open up' as they realise they are not going to be judged for what they say.

The third element is empathy – the understanding of what the client is saying and being able to 'step into their shoes'. It is important that the therapist communicates this understanding back to the client and therefore active listening is a very important part of the process.

Question time

How does this relate to social penetration theory? Can you see the links with rewards and costs?

Are any of the factors identified by Collins and Miller likely to affect this process?

What other factors might affect self-disclosure?

Mini plenary

Can you think of examples of social, psychological or cultural factors that influence self-disclosure in relationships? An example of each has been given below.

Psychological	Social	Cultural
Whether or not a person is looking for a long-term relationship.	Whether the relationship is romantic or not.	Whether the norms and values of that culture encourage or discourage disclosure.

AO3 (Analysis and evaluation of knowledge): How useful is this explanation?

How does culture affect self-disclosure?

One of the major issues studied in relation to cultural differences has been that of individualism vs collectivism and while some have argued that it is a false distinction (Takano and Osaka, 1999) and that these cultures are more alike than has previously been recognised, Tang et al. (2013) suggested that such differences were evident in sexual self-disclosure.

They reviewed previous research on the issue of self-disclosure and concluded that, on balance, there was evidence of differences between US and Chinese men and women in terms of self-disclosure, relating to sexual matters at least. In the US (individualistic) there was more disclosure concerning sexual thoughts and feelings than in China (collectivist).

This seems to provide evidence that culture is an important influence over the attractiveness of self-disclosure, as men and women in both cultures were satisfied with the level of self-disclosure provided. However, Chen and Nakazawa (2009) concluded that relational intimacy was also more of an issue, at least in intercultural relationships, than a simple idea of individualism vs collectivism. This suggests that cultural differences can be less of an issue when individuals have a strong sense of non-sexual closeness to each other. This aids the use of self-disclosure because with increased relational intimacy they are able to be more open and honest about all topics of conversation, regardless of cultural differences.

How does gender affect disclosure?

It is widely assumed that women will disclose more than men and the research referred to earlier (Collins and Miller, 1994) showed that there was a variety of research to support this view.

However, these stereotypical views may be changing, with a shift towards greater openness in society, leading to pressure on both genders to reveal more to their partners, which seems to suggest that this is regarded as not just required but attractive too.

Even as far back as the 1980s, Rubin et al. (1980), were able to show that the shift towards openness was having an effect. Using questionnaires with college student couples who were dating, they were able to show that very high proportions of both men and women had disclosed their thoughts and feelings fully in virtually all areas. However, they did find that women were more revealing in certain areas, including their greatest fears, and women were generally identified as the more highly disclosing partners. They also found that self-disclosure was strongly related to the respondents reported love for their partners and not to the power structure of their relationships.

This seems to suggest that although gender is a factor, social and cultural changes are affecting this and are likely to have had further effects since the 1980s, particularly with the advent of social media, which could not have been researched at that time.

How has social media changed self-disclosure in relationships?

The advent of social media has undoubtedly changed the nature, and certainly the amount, of information that we disclose to others, but has it changed the way that we respond to it and is it more or less attractive to disclose personal information online?

Recent research by Lee et al. (2019) has attempted to answer this question by studying nearly 400 adults (aged between 18 and 69). Using mock Facebook pages and self-report measures, they were able to identify the participants' attitudes towards both online and offline disclosures in relation to relation intimacy and satisfaction.

The overall finding was that although greater levels of self-disclosure are associated with higher relation intimacy and satisfaction in offline romantic relationships, the effect was the opposite in online romantic relationships. It may be worth noting that this effect was not true for non-romantic relationships and was only shown when the disclosures were perceived to have been made when the number of recipients included was high.

This seems to suggest that the effects of disclosure are related to the context in which they occur, and that disclosure carried out publicly, online, can be bad for romantic relationships and certainly not regarded as attractive. This links back to some of the factors identified by Collins and Miller (1994) related to appropriateness and attributions for disclosure in particular.

Is there a problem with causation in self-disclosure studies?

There is a wealth of research supporting the link between self-disclosure and higher levels of attraction/liking, using a range of participants (Lee et al., 2019), in different cultures (Chen and Nakazawa, 2009), in many types of relationships, suggesting that this notion is high in validity.

However, most of this research is based on correlational data, and so is able to establish a link between the two but not necessarily a causal relationship. This is because it is difficult to isolate self-disclosure from other variables that may also influence someone's attraction, for example similarity or physical attractiveness. Consequently, the validity of these findings has come into question.

However, the Collins and Miller (1994) research was a meta-analysis involving over 70 studies and thousands of participants, with a breakdown of different effects and situations in order to try to get over some of the confusion and unreliability that had emerged from previous studies. This clearly added to the validity of the findings, as similar effects were regularly shown in many different situations and with many different types of participants, and as such they were effectively able to show some of the other important variables involved (although culture was not one of them).

Mini plenary

Using the evaluation points above, try to evaluate the following statement:

Self-disclosure is always a way of increasing attractiveness in all relationships.

Arguments for	Arguments against

A modern issue – relationship disclosure on television, from Jerry Springer to Jeremy Kyle

How people open up to one another about their relationships was changed massively by television programmes such as *The Jerry Springer Show* in the US and *The Jeremy Kyle Show* in the UK. These programmes encouraged people to come on and bare all to their partners about very personal information, including their infidelity. Both shows have now been cancelled amid a high level of controversy.

New research

MAIL ONLINE

ITV axes The Jeremy Kyle Show *PERMANENTLY* over 'suicide' of grandfather 'humiliated' on show

By Mark Duell and Joseph Curtis

Published: 15 May 2019

The Jeremy Kyle Show has become the subject of an enquiry by MPs after the show was plunged into turmoil following the suicide of a man who has appeared on the show and been humiliated after failing a lie-detector test.

MPs have argued that programmes like this one are running the risk of putting people in danger when they had not suspected that such a thing could happen to them. They have further said that this kind of television which attracts millions of viewers has a responsibility to take care of its viewers and participants.

'With an increasing demand for this type of programming, we'll be examining broadcasting regulation in this area – is it fit for purpose?'

The show has been incredibly popular with over 3,000 episodes being made and many fans are predicting that it will go the same way as some presenters who have been sacked or banned in the past. Most believe that this will lead to a new forum for Kyle's style of television. E.g. 'JK Investigates' or 'The Kyle Show' would be possible titles and this kind of television is unlikely to be gone for long.

Question time

What does this suggest about self-disclosure as a factor in romantic relationships?

Why did people enjoy watching these programmes so much? Will they come back?

How closely does this relate to real life? Is it likely to have an effect on self-disclosure in the future?

Chapter plenary

1. What is meant by the term self-disclosure?
2. What is social penetration theory?
3. What is the breadth vs depth issue in self-disclosure?
4. What is meant by the rewards and costs of self-disclosure?
5. What are the other influences on self-disclosure?
6. How does self-disclosure link to humanistic psychology?
7. What is client-centred therapy?
8. What does this tell us about the use of self-disclosure in everyday life?
9. How might social and psychological factors influence self-disclosure?
10. How does culture influence self-disclosure?
11. How does gender influence self-disclosure?
12. How does social media affect self-disclosure in romantic relationships?
13. What is the causation problem in self-disclosure research?
14. What do TV shows like *Jeremy Kyle* tell us about the importance of self-disclosure in relationships?

Glossary

Key word	Definition
Active listening	Showing that you are fully listening to what someone is saying by responding appropriately.
Breadth vs depth	Breadth refers to a range of information covered without detail whereas depth refers to specific information being explored in more detail.
Congruence	When something is in harmony so that both are in agreement.
Empathy	The ability to understand the feelings of others.
Genuineness	Being absolutely true and honest, not acting or putting up a front.
Individualism vs collectivism	Individualism refers to cultures that are based on individual achievement and personal gain whereas collectivism refers to cultures that are based on collective achievement and the common good.
Meta-analysis	A method of research using data from a number of previous studies to try to establish an overall trend.
Reciprocity	Giving back what you have received from others.
Relational intimacy	The level of close, personal involvement between people in a relationship which is not usually related to sex.
Rewards and costs	Looking at the potential benefits and damages of an action.
Self-disclosure	A process of communication by which one person reveals information about themselves to another.
Stages of self-disclosure	Altman and Taylor identified different levels of penetration in a relationship that we go through as we become more intimate with a partner.
Trial and error	The process of experimenting with various methods of doing something until you find the most successful.
Unconditional positive regard	The acceptance and support of a person regardless of what the person says or does, especially in the context of client-centered therapy.

Plenary: Exam-style questions and answers with advisory comments

Question 1.

Explain what is meant by the term self-disclosure as a factor affecting attraction in relationships in psychology? [2 marks]

Marks for this question: AO1 = 2

Advice: In a question like this, it's important to make sure you are making it clear how this relates to psychology, so this will probably require an example. There is no need to provide any analysis or evaluation as both marks are for AO1: Knowledge and understanding.

Possible answer: Self-disclosure refers to the revealing of information from one person to another in a romantic relationship and it has been regarded as a possible factor in attraction in psychology by looking at the circumstances in which it will increase liking for someone, e.g. whether it's a good idea to reveal a lot of very personal information on a first date?

Question 2.

Chris and Ashley have been on two dates and Chris has decided to 'open up' to Ashley about previous relationships. Ashley is surprised by this and was intending to get to know Chris better before doing the same.

With reference to the section above, explain self-disclosure as a factor affecting attraction in romantic relationships. [4 marks]

Marks for this question: AO2 = 4

Advice: In this question, it's really important to recognise that all marks are for AO2, which means that you have to show the skill of application to the stem. You will still need to show an understanding of self-disclosure as a factor affecting attraction, but this time by picking out the references from the information you have been given. There is still no need to analyse or evaluate.

Possible answer: Self-disclosure is about revealing personal information and whether that leads to more or less liking by your partner in a romantic relationship. One factor that influences this is appropriateness: revealing too much too early (it's only the second date between Chris and Ashley) might decrease how much Ashley likes Chris. Another factor is content and, as this is about Chris's past relationships, it might make Ashley feel embarrassed or feel the need to reciprocate when it is clear that Ashley doesn't want to do that, at least not yet. Another factor is gender and there is evidence to show that different genders have different expectations about self-disclosure, so if Chris is male it might be surprising for him to be so open so soon and possibly lead to less liking, but it could also increase liking as it might suggest to Ashley that Chris wants to get closer and become more intimate.

Question 3.

Discuss self-disclosure as a factor affecting attraction in romantic relationships. [16 marks]

Marks for this question: AO1 = 6 and AO3 = 10

Advice: This question is looking for both skills of knowledge and understanding and analysis and evaluation. As there are 6 marks for AO1 and 10 for AO3, there should be greater emphasis on the evaluation. However, all such extended writing questions are marked holistically and therefore it is important that the knowledge is accurate and detailed and that the evaluation is clear and effective.

Possible answer: Self-disclosure is a factor affecting attraction as it is often suggested that revealing personal information to a romantic partner can increase feelings of liking and make the relationship more intimate.

Altman and Taylor suggested social penetration theory as a possible explanation for the effect of self-disclosure on attraction. They suggest that there is an issue of breadth versus depth and that self-disclosure in a relationship is like peeling back the layers of an onion, with the outer layers providing a broad idea of what someone is like, e.g. their work, family background, education, etc., and, as you get to know them and you get deeper into the inner layers, then you are able to find out more. The theory suggests that relationships go through stages and that as you get deeper into it then you become more intimate, so this suggests that attraction is linked to the increasing intimacy that comes from this disclosure.

They also suggest that individuals consider the rewards and costs of disclosure and they learn through trial and error to look out for the signs as to whether their disclosure is going to get a favourable reaction or not and whether their partner is going to reciprocate by disclosing information back to them.

Other factors that influence whether or not someone is going to disclose information to another were identified by Collins and Miller and they include, among others, the appropriateness of the disclosure: for example, it's generally suggested that you can give too much too soon, so talking about past relationships on a first date is probably too much. Another factor is gender, as it's often believed that women disclose more than men, and if the disclosure doesn't fit with that then it may lead to not liking rather than attraction. However, it is also argued that women might respond well to men disclosing, as it may seem unusual and therefore special. This relates to another factor identified by Collins and Miller, which is the attributions for the disclosure. This factor relates to the reasons that the disclosure is being given and if someone believes that the information is just intended for them then again this can make it seem more special and attractive than if it is deemed to be common knowledge. A final factor is the content of the disclosure, which, if it is something very personal, it can make the other person feel as though they have to reciprocate and therefore uncomfortable rather than attracted.

There are some areas where the need for self-disclosure is important and may need careful training, for example in the therapeutic arena where it can be extremely important that disclosure is carefully managed. One example of this is in Rogerian client-centred therapy, where genuineness on the part of the therapist is required in order to obtain a full understanding of the individual's problems. If the therapist comes across as acting or putting up a front this can have a bad effect and lead to the client holding back, in a similar way to what Altman and Taylor believed can happen when a romantic relationship breaks down.

Although social penetration theory and the factors identified by Collins and Miller do provide strong insights into how attraction can be understood in relation to self-disclosure, there are some influences that need to be considered in more depth, e.g. the influence of culture, gender, social media and individual differences.

Tang has shown that there are differences in sexual disclosure between US and Chinese men and women: in the US, which is traditionally regarded as an individualistic culture where individual recognition is important, sexual self-disclosure is higher than in China, a collectivist culture, where group recognition is more highly regarded. This suggests that previous research in this area may be suffering from a cultural bias as the differences identified by Tang had been ignored. However, Chen suggests that relational intimacy may be a more important factor in intercultural relationships than the traditional individualist vs collectivist distinction, particularly in intercultural relationships where otherwise there could be a clash between individualist and collectivist norms.

While gender has been identified as a factor by Collins and Miller, this may be based on stereotypical views that have changed over time. Even as far back as the 1980s, Rubin et al. showed that there was a new mood of openness, which meant that the traditional distinctions for gender-related levels of disclosure were not being maintained. Using questionnaires with dating couples, they found that both men and women disclosed their feelings fully and that this seemed to fit with what was expected at the time. Consequently, this suggested that changes in society were having an effect and indicated a lack of temporal validity and, of course, the advent of social media is likely to further change these influences.

Using self-report measures and mock Facebook pages, Lee et al. were able to show that although high levels of self-disclosure were linked to higher levels of intimacy offline, this was not the same for information disclosed online. This relates well to some of the factors identified by Collins and Miller, particularly regarding the attributions for disclosure, as information disclosed on social media may be regarded as too public – therefore the context of the disclosure is important too.

Unfortunately, most of the research in this area is correlational, which may show a link between self-disclosure and liking but it is not showing a causal link and as such the validity must be questioned. However, there is a wealth of research into this that shows similar effects in many different types of relationships so the validity shouldn't be completely dismissed.

Altman, I. and Taylor, D.A. (1973) *Social Penetration: The Development of Interpersonal Relationships*. New York: Holt, Rinehart & Winston.

Chen, Y.W. and Nakazawa, M. (2009) Influences of culture on self-disclosure as relationally situated in intercultural and interracial friendships from a social penetration perspective. *Journal of Intercultural Communication Research*, 38 (2): 77–98.

Collins, N.L. and Miller, L.C. (1994) Self-disclosure and liking: A meta-analytic review. *Psychological Bulletin*, 116 (3): 457.

Duell, M. and Curtiss, J. (2019) ITV axes *The Jeremy Kyle Show* PERMANENTLY over 'suicide' of grandfather 'humiliated' on show. *Mail Online*. 15 May 2019.

Jourard, S.M. (1959) Self-disclosure and other-cathexis. *The Journal of Abnormal and Social Psychology*, 59 (3): 428.

Lee, J., Gillath, O. and Miller, A. (2019) Effects of self- and partner's online disclosure on relationship intimacy and satisfaction. *PLOS One*, 14 (3): e0212186.

Rogers, C.R. (1995 [1980]) *A Way of Being*. New York: Houghton Mifflin Harcourt.

Rubin, Z., Hill, C.T., Peplau, L.A. and Dunkel-Schetter, C. (1980) Self-disclosure in dating couples: Sex roles and the ethic of openness. *Journal of Marriage and the Family*, 1 May, pp. 305–317.

Takano, Y. and Osaka, E. (1999) An unsupported common view: Comparing Japan and the US on individualism/collectivism. *Asian Journal of Social Psychology*, 2 (3): 311–341.

Tang, N., Bensman, L. and Hatfield, E. (2013). Culture and sexual self-disclosure in intimate relationships. *Interpersona*, 7 (2): 227.

Chapter 4
Factors affecting romantic relationships 2: Physical attractiveness

Spec check

Factors affecting attraction in romantic relationships: physical attractiveness

AO1 (Knowledge and understanding): Factors affecting romantic relationships: physical attractiveness

'Beauty is in the eye of the beholder' is a phrase that has been used in some form or other for centuries. It essentially suggests that what is regarded as beautiful differs from one person to another and therefore it's not possible to say that someone is physically attractive as they are only likely to be physically attractive to some people and not to others. But is that really true? We would all like to think that we judge people on more than just physical features, but do we? Or are we just kidding ourselves and we really know that we prefer some people over others just because of the way they look?

Think!

Do you prefer the look of a certain type of person? Are there certain features that you regard as important?

Do you believe in love at first sight and if so, what is that makes this happen?

It is likely that if you believe in love at first sight then you will be judging someone based on their looks rather than their personality, particularly if you haven't actually met the person. Prince Harry claimed that he fell in love with Meghan Markle 'the very first time we met' (BBC interview, 27 November 2017), but is this the same as saying 'the first time I saw her'? When you meet someone, you make judgements about what a person says and how they respond, rather than just what they look like, although it probably helped that she was regarded as one of the most beautiful women on the planet?

What do we mean by physical attractiveness?

There are many features that have been studied to identify what makes someone attractive and there is definitely no single factor, but much of the research suggests that some of the following are important.

Facial symmetry (both sides of the face look the same), averageness (look like most others), unblemished skin, youthfulness, positive expressions, feminine features in women (oval face, etc.) and masculine features in men (square jaw, etc.). Alongside this, there is plenty of research to suggest that certain body shapes are more attractive, although this differs for men and women as shown by the perceived ideal waist-to-hip ratio in women being 0.7 and for men 0.9.

All of these features seem to have some relationship with a judgement of how healthy someone is and possibly how likely they are to produce healthy offspring. And all this suggests that physical attractiveness is an important factor, not just in terms of whether we judge someone to be the person we want to have sex with but also in terms of whether we judge that person to be good or bad.

The halo effect

People who are physically attractive are often judged to be have other positive characteristics too, the 'beauty is good' heuristic is a cognitive bias that creates a view that attractive people must also be good people, and therefore we place a metaphorical halo above their heads, which gives them the status of a 'god-like' figure suggesting that they can do no wrong.

In an early study of the halo effect, Dion et al. (1972) were able to show how strongly a person's judgements can be affected by someone's looks when they gave their participants nothing more than photographs of people (who had been previously peer-rated on their attractiveness) and asked them to assign other traits to them. The findings were extraordinary, in that the positive traits were assigned to the people thought to be more attractive, who were also judged to be happier and more successful and even judged to be better parents!

Question time

What do these findings tell us about physical attractiveness? Is it just about lust/sex?

What other judgements are we making when seeing someone as physically attractive?

How does this relate to long-term relationships?

It seems clear that physical attractiveness is linked to our desire for a partner who is not just beautiful on the outside but on the inside too. If we make the 'beauty is good' assumption, then we must be hoping that this will be the sort of person we would like to have a proper relationship with and not just a one-night stand.

However, our judgement of someone else as a potential mate might also be influenced by our judgement of our own level of physical attractiveness and to what extent we would make a good match.

The matching hypothesis

In spite of the cognitive bias outlined above, it has also been argued that we approach relationships in a logical manner and make an assessment of our own level of attractiveness when looking for a long-term partner. According to the matching hypothesis (Walster et al., 1966), this assessment encourages us to be more realistic in our choice and consequently look for someone who matches our level of attractiveness. This is regarded as not only more realistic but also likely to be more successful when considering someone for a long-term relationship. This doesn't just mean that we are accepting that we should choose some who is unattractive but that, in making this assessment, we come to see others who are similar to ourselves as at least attractive enough. A big part of this realism is in the need to ensure that we choose someone who will stay with us and as such our choice is motivated by the desire to avoid rejection and the potential breakdown of the relationship.

Question time

Do you know couples who don't match in terms of physical attractiveness? Are they the exception or the rule?

Is it realistic to judge some people as 'out of your league', when thinking of starting a relationship?

How does this affect the importance of physical attractiveness in attraction to someone? Does it mean that it's more or less important?

Mini plenary

Explain three reasons why physical attractiveness is important in relationships.

AO2 (Application of knowledge): How does this apply in practice?

Beauty and the brain

Neuroscience has allowed researchers to identify parts of the brain involved in many forms of activity and this is certainly true of our assessment of physical attractiveness. Most of the research has suggested support for an evolutionary view and as such has suggested that there are differences in the parts of the brain used by males and females in judging physical attractiveness.

In a review of research into this area, Yarosh (2019) suggested that research had shown specific areas of the brain involved in the perception of beauty. The areas identified were the orbitofrontal cortex (OFC), the nucleus accumbens (involved in making judgements of beauty) and the ventromedial prefrontal cortex (vmPFC), which in male subjects is more sensitive to physical attributes, such as the youthfulness and gender of faces, than in female subjects.

This suggests a degree of localisation in the brain similar to that found for other forms of human behaviour such as speech (Broca's area and Wernicke's area) and therefore it could be that our judgement of beauty is indeed built into our brain.

Interleave me now

Brain localisation

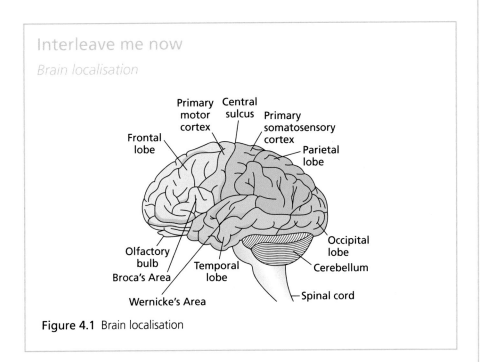

Figure 4.1 Brain localisation

Question time

What does localisation tell us about physical attractiveness?

If our perception of attractiveness is built into our brain, what does that tell us about the **nature–nurture debate**?

Can an awareness of our tendency to judge attractiveness in the ways suggested have any effect on our behaviour?

How do the issues and debates identified below relate to the influence of physical attractiveness?

Can you think of how another debate might be relevant?

Nature–nurture	Gender bias	Culture bias	Another debate

AO3 (Analysis and evaluation of knowledge): How useful is this explanation?

Does the halo effect make us judge attractive people as more intelligent?

The halo effect seems to make us judge attractive people in many areas that have no relationship to our looks. One area where this is most pronounced is in the area of intelligence and academic performance. There should be no necessary connection between physical attractiveness and intelligence and yet some research has shown that it can make us predict better future academic performance for those that have it.

Talamas et al. (2016) used pictures of 100 Caucasian university students aged 18–24 and asked over 100 volunteers to rate both their physical attractiveness and perceived academic performance. They wanted to see if the rating of attractiveness was positively correlated with perceived academic performance, this was then compared to the actual academic performance of the original 100 students to check for accuracy.

As predicted, there was no relationship between attractiveness and actual academic performance ($r = 0.03$), but there were strong positive correlations between attractiveness and perceived intelligence ($r = 0.81$) and attractiveness and perceived academic performance ($r = 0.74$).

This suggests that the halo effect is real and makes people believe all sorts of things about attractive people, even things that should have no connection to being attractive such as intelligence. This has been supported by many studies finding similar results and suggests that there is high validity in these findings and, even more than that, strong support for the idea that physical attractiveness is a major factor in what people are looking for in a relationship.

How does culture affect physical attractiveness?

Some research has suggested that there are cultural differences in judgements of attractiveness. Wheeler and Kim (1997), for example, found that participants in the collectivistic culture of Korea had different stereotypes of attractiveness to participants in the individualistic culture of the US, such that Koreans tended to link attractiveness to concern for others and harmonious relationships while Americans tended to link attractiveness to strength and assertiveness.

However, this still suggests that both cultures had a clear idea of what attractiveness is and in a meta-analysis of over 900 studies looking into the reliability of measures of attractiveness, Langlois et al. (2000) found that there was significant consistency in judgements of attractiveness across cultures.

They reviewed as many studies as they could find that looked at physical attractiveness in any way and found that there was remarkable consistency in how attractiveness was judged, and this included measures from different cultures.

This seems to suggest that culture does play a role in the traits that are subsequently assigned to attractive people, so that different cultures seem to have different ideas of what they regard as positive and negative traits. However, this doesn't seem to take away from the fact that what is regarded as facially attractive seems to be the same across all cultures, suggesting that facial attractiveness at least, is universal.

Do we avoid people who are 'out of our league'?

If the matching hypothesis is correct then we should not bother trying to form relationships with people who are much more attractive than ourselves, however much we fancy them. Instead we should just settle for the best that we can get.

While there is plenty of anecdotal evidence to support this notion, there is little empirical evidence showing it to be true and the evidence that is available is generally correlational and based on artificial scenarios, which tend to lack ecological validity.

Shaw Taylor et al. (2011) attempted to redress this with a study that was based around an analysis of choices made by people on real online dating sites. They used the profiles of 60 heterosexual males and 60 heterosexual females and all of their contacts to provide independent assessors with 966 photos that were then assessed for attractiveness. They compared the attractiveness of their sample with the attractiveness of those people they had attempted to contact and did the same for those that responded and didn't respond.

Their findings were that people generally tried to contact someone who was more attractive than themselves, showing no evidence of matching, which suggests that people's judgements of themselves do not play a large part in their attraction to others as they are generally trying to get the most attractive person they can. However, they did find some evidence of matching in the response to attempted contact as more attractive people tended to not respond to less attractive people so that the participants ended up with someone with a similar level of attractiveness, almost by accident!

This might help explain why there are many anecdotal examples of matching – people tend to end up with someone who is of a similar level of attractiveness because that was the person who responded to their initial contact, be that online or in some other way. It's not that people aren't trying to get someone more attractive than them, it's just that they are failing to achieve it. Matching does occur, but not by choice.

Is the perception of attractiveness with us from birth?

If very young infants show a preference for attractive faces, does that suggest that our judgement of attractiveness is innate and therefore not influenced by nurturing or environmental factors?

This was the idea tested by Hoss and Langlois (2003) at the University of Texas with 6-month-old infants using a preferential-looking technique. The infants were presented with two pictures side by side, which had previously been rated as one being attractive and the other unattractive, and the time spent looking at each picture was measured. If the infants spent longer looking at one rather than the other, they could be said to prefer it.

Not only did Hoss and Langlois find that the 6-month-olds preferred looking at the more attractive picture, but when they repeated the experiment with 2 – month olds they found similar results, suggesting that our perception of attractiveness is innate and so not formed gradually through a process of learning.

This provides some evidence for the view that perceptions of attractiveness are the same for everyone and that we have a natural preference for certain kinds of faces, particularly when you take into account the fact that the researchers had gone to some lengths to ensure that other potential confounding variables, such as hair colour and length, facial expression, etc., were dealt with as far as possible in order to ensure that the only difference between the two pictures was the rated facial attractiveness. Hopefully this, alongside the fact that they were using a measure of preference that has been used in many previous studies, makes their findings more valid.

Mini plenary

How important is physical attractiveness when looking for a potential romantic partner?

Try to answer this question in no more than 150 words, using the evaluation points above.

A modern issue – the use of physical attractiveness on TV dating programmes

Selecting and attracting a mate is a constant issue for all species and as such it's not surprising that TV programme-makers have got involved with programmes such as *Blind Date* and *Take Me Out*, which have been able to cash in on the fascination that we all have with what makes a good relationship. However, the question of whether it is looks or personality that are important is not particularly focused on in these shows.

New research

INDEPENDENT ONLINE

Naked attraction: what nakedness can reveal about a potential partner

By Gayle Brewer

Wednesday 24 August 2016 15: 27

Channel 4 has taken TV dating much further than it has ever gone before with the introduction of the TV show *Naked Attraction*. In the show, contestants appear entirely naked and have sections of their body revealed to potential partners, who then decide which one they like the 'look' of.

Physical features, such as their body shape, genital size, bodily hair, teeth quality and presence or otherwise of tattoos are discussed in order to help them reach a decision. Although this type of scrutiny is unusual for a TV show, it does reflect in some ways the importance of physical appearance in these kinds of decisions.

Such features may be more than just superficial as they can indicate certain health conditions, e.g. body shape may give clues about the person's likelihood of developing heart disease, unusual teeth spacing can be an indication of genetic disorders, such as Rapp-Hodgkin syndrome. So, if you're looking for a healthy partner, asking them to get naked before you get into a relationship might be the way to go.

Question time

What does this suggest about physical attractiveness as a factor in romantic relationships?

Is this programme purely designed to create interest and publicity by shock tactics? Would you watch it? If not, why not?

How closely does this relate to real life?

Chapter plenary

1. Is there such a thing as love at first sight?
2. What is meant by physical attractiveness?
3. What is the Halo Effect?
4. What is the Matching Hypothesis?
5. Are our ideas of beauty located somewhere in our brain?
6. What is meant by brain localisation?
7. Why is there a nature–nurture debate in relation to physical attractiveness?
8. What is the nature view?

9. What is the nurture view?

10. Does the halo effect make us judge attractive people as more intelligent?

11. Are there cultural differences in the judgement of physical attractiveness?

12. Is there evidence for the matching hypothesis?

13. Is perception of attractiveness with us from birth?

14. Do TV programmes like Naked Attraction help in our choice of romantic partner?

Glossary

Key word	Definition
Anecdotal evidence	This is information in the form of stories that people tell about what has happened to them or what they have seen. There is no way of knowing if it's true or not.
Collectivistic culture	Societies that are based on collective achievement and the common good.
Empirical evidence	This is information acquired by scientific observation or experimentation.
Facial symmetry	Having similar proportions on both sides of the face so that both sides look alike.
Halo effect	The tendency for an impression created in one area to influence opinion in another area.
Individualistic culture	Societies that are based on individual achievement and personal gain.
Innate	Something that is present at birth.
Love at first sight	The experience of falling in love with someone as soon as you see them for the first time.
Matching hypothesis	This refers to the prediction that people will be attracted to, and form relationships with, individuals who are of a similar level of attractiveness to them.
Nature–nurture debate	The extent to which human behaviour is innate and therefore part of our biological inheritance or learned from our environmental influences.
Nucleus accumbens	This is a region in the basal forebrain near to the front of the preoptic area of the hypothalamus, particularly important in the reward system of the brain.

Key word	Definition
Orbitofrontal cortex (OFC)	The area of the cerebral cortex located at the base of the frontal lobes above the eye sockets, involved especially in social and emotional behaviour.
Out of your league	A comparison to sporting teams who are in different leagues and suggests that someone is too good for someone else.
Ventromedial prefrontal cortex (vmPFC)	This is in the frontal lobe at the bottom of the cerebral hemispheres and is involved in the processing of risk and fear.
Waist-to-hip ratio	This is calculated as waist measurement divided by hip measurement. For example, a person with a 28" waist and 38" hips has a waist-to-hip ratio of 0.7.

Plenary: Exam-style questions and answers with advisory comments

Question 1.

Explain what is meant by the matching hypothesis as a factor affecting attraction in relationships in psychology? [2 marks]

Marks for this question: AO1 = 2

Advice: In a question like this, it's important to make sure you are making it clear how it relates to psychology, so it will probably require an example. There is no need to provide any analysis or evaluation as both marks are for AO1: Knowledge and understanding.

Possible answer: The matching hypothesis refers to the prediction that someone will be attracted to and try to form a relationship with someone who is of a similar level of attractiveness to themselves. This was first put forward by Walster who believed that people do it in order to avoid rejection or out of fear that the other person won't stay with them if they are 'out of their league'.

Question 2.

The idea that 'beauty is in the eye of the beholder' is an old phrase that suggests that what is regarded as physically attractive is different from one person to the next. The perception of beauty therefore is more to do with individual experiences rather than linked to something in the brain. If this is true, we would expect to find that people would be choosing romantic partners of different levels of attractiveness depending on their personal preference, rather than looking for the stereotypical beauty!

With reference to the section above, discuss physical attractiveness as a factor affecting attraction in romantic relationships. [16 marks]

Marks for this question: AO1 = 6, AO2 = 4 and AO3 = 6

Advice: This question is looking for all three skills of: knowledge and understanding; application of knowledge; and analysis and evaluation. As there are 6 marks for AO1 and 6 for AO3, there should be a roughly equal emphasis on knowledge and understanding and evaluation. However, with 4 marks for AO2 on this question, there is also the need for significant reference to the material in the stem. It's important to ensure that you have shown the examiner that you have applied your knowledge to the stem, so it's always a good idea to use some of the words/sentences/phrases from the stem.

Possible answer: The first impression that we get of a prospective romantic partner is likely to be what they look like. When you see someone across a crowded room or their picture on a dating website, you will make a judgement about that person. The first judgement you are likely to make concerns whether or not their face looks nice and whether or not you find it attractive.

Evolutionary arguments have suggested that there are certain facial characteristics that everyone finds attractive, such as youthfulness or facial symmetry, as well as some that are specific to your gender, such as an oval face for women and a square jaw for men. If this is true, then it would suggest that physical attractiveness is not 'in the eye of the beholder' as suggested above but is in fact natural and the same for everyone.

The section above suggests that the perception of attractiveness may not be linked to something happening in the brain, however, it could be that this perception is localised in the brain in the same way as other areas of the brain are responsible for speech or for memory, so we could have a section of the brain linked to beauty.

In a review of research into the neuroscience of attraction, Yarosh identified areas of the brain believed to be involved in the perception of beauty as the orbitofrontal cortex and the nucleus accumbens, which might provide support for the idea that attractiveness is a natural factor and therefore affects us all in the same way. Therefore, suggesting that attractiveness isn't a matter of 'personal preference', as suggested above, but an in-built mechanism that's the same for everyone.

Further evidence for the idea that physical attractiveness is innate comes from a study of infant preferences for attractive faces conducted by Hoss and Langlois. They showed 6-month-old infants two pictures of faces, one of which had been previously rated as attractive with the other being rated as unattractive. They found that the infants preferred to look at the attractive face rather than the unattractive face (measured by how long they spent looking at the face), suggesting that our preference for attractive faces is innate and that our judgement of attractiveness is universal. It could of course, be argued that by 6 months the infants had learned to like certain types of faces ore and that this fitted with the stereotypes used by the raters. However, the research was extended to include 2–3 month–old infants who displayed the same preferences, providing further evidence that a preference for certain types of facial characteristics that are generally regarded as attractive is innate and not down to 'individual experiences', as suggested above.

The matching hypothesis in psychology suggests that our choice of romantic partner is influenced by our own level of attractiveness and predicts that we will choose someone of a similar level to ourselves. According to Walster et al., we do this in order to avoid rejection and to attempt to ensure that the person we choose will stay with us in the long term, and they will not be looking for someone else who is more attractive. This seems to go against the statement above, which suggests that we 'would be choosing partners with different levels of attractiveness'. Although if it is based on experience, as also suggested above, then that might fit in with the direction suggested by the hypothesis that they have learned from experience what happens if you go for someone 'out of your league'.

Much of the evidence for the matching hypothesis has been anecdotal in so far as many people will tell you stories of people they know or have seen who seem to have similar levels of attractiveness. However, Shaw Taylor et al. attempted to provide empirical evidence to test the hypothesis in an analysis of online dating websites. They used profiles from 60 male and 60 female members of dating websites and gained access to all their contacts on the site. Having used independent assessors to rate both the attractiveness of the members and that of their contacts, they found no support for the idea that the participants tended to go for people of a similar level of attractiveness, finding instead that they tended to go for people of a higher level. However, they did find that the people with whom the participants were successful did tend to have a similar level of attractiveness, suggesting that matching isn't a strong influence on attachment but that it does happen by accident. This might help to explain the anecdotal evidence as many people might see those with similar attractiveness forming relationships, even though they actually wanted to form a relationship with someone better looking than themselves.

Whether we are biologically programmed to find some people attractive or socially pressured into believing that certain features are attractive, it may be that an awareness of this would be useful in order to help prevent people being labelled as unattractive and suffering the kind of stigma that goes with that label. This might help to prevent the kind of mental health and social problems that arise when people are judging who is and isn't worthy of interest in society.

References

Brewer, G. (2016) Naked attraction: What nakedness can reveal about a potential partner. *Independent Online*, 24 August 2016.

Dion, K., Berscheid, E. and Walster, E. (1972) What is beautiful is good. *Journal of Personality and Social Psychology*, 24 (3): 285.

Hoss, R.A. and Langlois, J.H. (2003) Infants prefer attractive faces. In O. Pascalis and A. Slater (eds), *The Development of Face Processing in Infancy and Early Childhood: Current Perspectives* New York: Nova Science Publishers, pp. 27–38.

Langlois, J.H., Kalakanis, L., Rubenstein, A.J., Larson, A., Hallam, M. and Smoot, M. (2000) Maxims or myths of beauty? A meta-analytic and theoretical review. *Psychological Bulletin*, 126 (3): 390.

Shaw Taylor, L., Fiore, A.T., Mendelsohn, G.A. and Cheshire, C. (2011) 'Out of my league': A real-world test of the matching hypothesis. *Personality and Social Psychology Bulletin*, 37 (7): 942–954.

Talamas, S.N., Mavor, K.I. and Perrett, D.I. (2016) Blinded by beauty: Attractiveness bias and accurate perceptions of academic performance. *PloS One*, 11 (2): e0148284.

Walster, E., Aronson, V., Abrahams, D. and Rottman, L. (1966) Importance of physical attractiveness in dating behavior. *Journal of Personality and Social Psychology*, 4 (5): 508.

Wheeler, L. and Kim, Y. (1997). What is beautiful is culturally good: The physical attractiveness stereotype has different content in collectivistic cultures. *Personality and Social Psychology Bulletin*, 23 (8): 795–800.

Yarosh, D.B. (2019). Perception and deception: Human beauty and the brain. *Behavioral Sciences*, 9 (4): 34.

Chapter 5
Factors affecting romantic relationships 3: Filter theory

Spec check

Factors affecting attraction in romantic relationships: filter theory

AO1 (Knowledge and understanding): Factors affecting romantic relationships: filter theory

What is the basis of filter theory?

When you think of a filter, you might think of something that removes certain properties from a substance (usually the unwanted ones) but still leaves behind all of the desirable properties, like a water filter. Alternatively, you might think of something that helps to narrow something down in order to make it more manageable, like the neck of a bottle. Both of these could be applied to filter theory in the way that it explains how we apply filters to relationships.

According to Kerckhoff and Davis (1962), when we are selecting a partner we have a wide range of people available to us (sometimes called a field of eligibles), from which we need to choose just one! Consequently, in order to make this choice, we first need to decide what criteria we are going to set and how we are going to eliminate certain people from the field. Kerckhoff and Davis suggest that our criteria are formed into a series of filters that help us to narrow the field down and some of these filters are particularly important.

Think!

If you were going to attempt to choose a partner from the whole population, how would you go about narrowing down the field?

Would you focus on physical attractiveness first or would there be other criteria that would make your search more manageable and realistic?

Filter 1: Social demography

Demography refers to the structure of the population and social demography refers to the social characteristics of people in the population, such as age, ethnicity, social class, educational level and, importantly, geographical location. All of these play some part in the decision over who to choose as a partner, because if they are too far away from the kind of person we are, which could literally be miles away in the case of geographical location, then we are less likely to find anything in common or even meet in the first place. This first filter should narrow the field down considerably and allow a person to move on to other potential issues, having hopefully met some of the eligible partners. The term homogamy is used to describe how we are likely to come together in a relationship with someone who is socially or culturally similar to ourselves and this first filter helps us to achieve this.

Filter 2: Similarity in attitudes

This is concerned with the extent to which people agree over the opinions they hold and whether they fit in with the people they are trying to form a relationship with. Once people have met (having used the first filter successfully), they are likely to have conversations about what each person thinks about this or that. If they find that their attitudes and values are completely at odds with one another, then this will lead to disagreement and it's unlikely that the relationship will continue for long. It's not the case that couples have to agree over everything, but broad agreement over important values and opinions definitely helps.

Filter 3: Complementarity

This filter is concerned with the extent to which romantic partners meet each other's needs and is likely to occur at a later stage in the relationship than the other two. The focus here is more on heterogamy as people need someone who has different personal attributes to their own in order to make up for something that they lack. If two people have the same kind of personal characteristics then they may find it difficult to cope. For example, if both are very organised but not able to adapt to new situations then this will make it difficult to meet new and unusual challenges; whereas if each one has a different quality, then they are more likely to complement each other and form a unit that possesses the skills and abilities to cope in the long run.

Question time

Are these filters really about attraction and romance or something else?

Are there any other filters that you think are missing?

Are these filters more important than physical attractiveness and self-disclosure?

The question of what *are* love and romance is raised when going through these filters, as they don't appear to be very romantic! If we are to believe the stories told about romance in books and films, then we would have star-crossed lovers overcoming all the obstacles and living happily ever after. But I guess real life isn't quite like that, and these filters are at least realistic in their view of who you are likely to meet and stay with for any length of time. As boring as it sounds, real life does indeed throw up lots of challenges, and using these filters might well help people stay together – although considering the high divorce rate, perhaps not everyone is using them as well as they should.

Mini plenary

One of the statements in the list below describes the social demography filter, one describes the similarity in attitudes filter and one describes the complementarity filter. Place the correct letter next to each of the named filters below the list to indicate which of the statements fit with each filter (the other two statements don't relate to any of these filters).

A – Helps to filter out those people who have very different opinions to ourselves.
B – Helps to filter out those people we do not find good looking.
C – Helps to filter out those people who live too far away.
D – Helps to filter out those people who don't meet our needs.
E – Helps to filter out those people who aren't prepared to talk openly about their past.

☐ Social demography filter.
☐ Similarity in attitudes filter.
☐ Complementarity filter.

AO2 (Application of knowledge): How does this apply in practice?

Filter theory and the cognitive approach

The cognitive approach in psychology suggests that we spend our lives attempting to deal with an incredible amount of incoming information – we are literally bombarded with information. In this situation, our minds have to try to process this information in order to make sense of it. One of the ways that we do this is through a process of filtering out information that we don't need, to ensure that only the material that is important to us gets through. The bottleneck metaphor has been used to explain this process of narrowing down the information coming in until we get to the information that we require.

Too much information –
How do we select what's relevant?

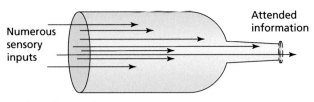

Bottleneck metaphor

Figure 5.1 The bottleneck metaphor

Interleave me now

Psychopathology and filter theory

The cognitive approach to psychopathology argues that mental disorders result from faulty processing and therefore a distortion of the information that is coming into us. Aaron Beck had the view that mental disorders, particularly depression, were caused by these kinds of cognitive distortions, leading to negative and irrational thinking.

Cognitive distortions

Cognitive distortions are biased views we take on ourselves and the world around us. They are irrational thoughts and beliefs that we unknowingly reinforce over time. One such distortion is the mental filter.

Mental filter

Similar to overgeneralisation, the mental filter focuses on a single negative and excludes all the positive. An example of this distortion is one partner in a *romantic relationship* dwelling on a single negative comment made by the other partner and viewing the relationship as hopelessly lost, while ignoring the years of positive comments and experiences. The mental filter can foster a negative view of everything around a person by focusing only on the negative.

Question time

How does the cognitive approach use filters? Is it the same as Kerckhoff and Davis's use of filters?

Are filters always useful in romantic relationships?

Lee and Lesley met in a local pub and, having lived together as a couple for 18 months, lots of people have been encouraging them to get married, but neither Lee nor Lesley think marriage is that important. What they do find important is how well they work together in their relationship, Lee is a very good listener and is good at dealing with any stressful situations that they face, whereas Lesley is better at dealing with practical things like organising their holidays.

Using the material above, explain how the three filters of filter theory would explain the success of Lee and Lesley's relationship.

AO3 (Analysis and evaluation of knowledge): How useful is this explanation?

Is there homogamy in all relationships?

The idea that people with similar social characteristics are more likely to meet and get together has face validity as it seems both logical and (almost) common sense. How would people meet in the first place if not local/involved in similar activities? How would they make any kind of connection if they didn't have similar characteristics? However, it is questionable whether this is true for all kinds of relationships.

Lin et al. (2019) carried out demographic research comparing these social characteristics in same-sex and different-sex couples in Taiwan. This was done to provide evidence of the similarities and differences between these two types of relationships in a non-Western context. They found that although many of the factors associated with relationship formation and break-up are the same for same-sex and different-sex relationships, same-sex relationships are actually more homogamous in terms of age and education level than different-sex ones. This provides support for the filter theory as the effect of certain social characteristics was very clear.

However, they also found that same-sex relationships were more heterogamous in terms of family economic background than different-sex relationships, which provides evidence *against* filter theory for these social characteristics. Suggesting that filter theory may be overgeneralising the effect of all social characteristics and in fact it may be that certain characteristics are more important than others. Furthermore, the evidence above suggests that both cultural and sexual orientation factors are important in determining the formation of relationships, which wasn't taken into account in the original theory.

Has filter theory got cause and effect the wrong way round?

Another aspect of filter theory that seems to make sense is the argument that once couples have met, it is their similarities in values and attitudes that will help them develop their relationship, as without this agreement the relationship is unlikely to last. However, it could be that similarity is something that develops as a result of being together rather than being important in bringing people together.

Anderson et al. (2003) conducted a study of dating partners at the beginning of their relationship and again, at least 6 months later, looking at their responses to discussions of emotional topics such as a recent concern or worry. They found that a process of *emotional convergence* occurred in which the emotional responses of partners became more similar over the period studied.

It seems as though romantic partners become more tuned into one another and more similar over the course of their relationship, and therefore it is the effect of being together that brings about this similarity, rather than it being the cause of the relationship developing in the first place.

Filter theory therefore, seems to have got cause and effect the wrong way round in the belief that it is similarity in attitudes that brings people together, although in a broader sense, it seems Kerckhoff and Davis (1962) were right to stress the importance of this similarity, as Anderson et al. have shown that it is an important factor in keeping relationships together in the long term whichever way round it happens.

Does the rise of internet dating mean that filter theory is out of date?

One of the criticisms that is often levelled at psychological research conducted more than 50 years ago, like that of Kerckhoff and Davis is that it lacks temporal validity, as it no longer applies to the modern world. Relationship formation and dating has certainly changed a lot since their theory was developed and internet dating with mobile apps like Tinder and websites like Match.com have certainly made people from a wide variety of backgrounds and geographical locations available to others in a way never experienced in the 1960s. However, is it true to say that this means that people are using these kinds of filters less than they used to or more?

Dating websites and apps have indeed created the possibility of meeting a lot more people, but in some ways this means that there is a need to be *more* selective, after all, if you don't like the look or sound of one, there are always 'plenty more fish' in the sea (if you'll forgive the pun). Consequently, internet daters are faced with the need to decide who to meet and who not to meet on a regular basis and this makes their 'filtering' even more important.

Mantell (2018) argues that internet dating can be compared to a military operation in which drones are deployed to search for a target, such is the need to 'filter out' those that don't fit the requirements of the potential dater. Mantell also suggests that the process of filtering is even more demanding than in other forms of relationships, at least partially because of the tendency of users to hold back information (or lie as it is sometimes called).

Other research, e.g. Couch and Liamputtong (2008), found a similar kind of filtering in internet dating, particularly in terms of geographical location for some but not all users, supporting the social demography aspect of filter theory. However, most of the research into internet dating still finds that physical attractiveness is of utmost importance and one of the things that preoccupies the thoughts of most potential daters is the possibility that any pictures provided are out of date or just false. Therefore, it may be that it is physical attractiveness that is the most important factor in attraction rather than any other social or value concerns.

Do opposites complement each other in a long-term relationship?

Filter theory suggests that whilst it is important to have similar attitudes and values in the development of a relationship, in the long term it's complementary skills that keep a relationship going. So, is it possible that those so similar can also end up being different enough to keep a relationship going? Research from Bohns et al. (2013) suggests that it just might.

Their research suggests that similarity and complementarity may each be beneficial within a restricted range of contexts: similarity may be particularly useful for establishing agreement on joint goals and avoiding conflict, while complementarity may be advantageous in situations where two individuals are already in agreement and are now concerned with interpersonal coordination and goal pursuit.

It seems that it's important to have one person in a relationship who's being vigilant and making sure that what the other person is eagerly jumping into isn't going to cause problems for the future. In this way it's possible for both to be heading in the same direction and to have the same goals but with enough checks and balances to be sure that things work well for both.

There seems to be some validity in the claim of complementarity made by Kerckhoff and Davis, and this time it isn't just face validity but actual support from other research.

<hr>

Mini plenary

What is the evidence for and against filter theory? Try to 'filter' through the evaluation points above and decide which support filter theory and which oppose it.

Supports filter theory	Opposes filter theory

The need to filter through a range of 'eligibles' clearly isn't easy, and it doesn't seem as though the internet is making it any easier. One solution might be to be able to meet someone without too much pressure and with the ability to walk away or just cross them off your list. So, is speed dating the answer?

New research

THE NUTTY TALKS – LIFESTYLE

My first speed dating experience

By B.K. Advtravlr

Published 3 June 2018

Having tried all sorts of dating, including online, I decided it was time to give speed dating a go, partially to see what all the fuss is about, but also just because it's a good idea to have new experiences and who knows something really good might come of it.

Day of the event

Having arrived early, which is unusual, finding that the idea that women arrive fashionably late was completely true, I decided to go and talk to the only woman, apart from the host, who was there and see what she was like.

My approach to the whole process can be summed up in the following points:

1. Be complementary about her looks or clothes.
2. Find out what she is looking for in a guy.
3. Ask about three interesting topics that she wants to talk about.
4. Follow up each one with further enquiries about it.
5. Don't disagree with anything she says.

Conclusion

This was definitely preferable to online dating for someone looking for a serious relationship. In speed dating you get to see what the person looks like and can find out a lot more about them and make a more informed judgement. It's not right for everyone, but it is a step in the right direction!

Chapter plenary

1. What is the basis of filter theory?
2. What is meant by social demography?
3. What is meant by similarity of attitudes?
4. What is meant by complementarity?
5. How do the three filters explain forming, developing and maintaining relationships?
6. What does the cognitive approach say about filters?
7. How does filter theory apply to psychopathology?
8. How closely is the filter theory of romantic relationships related to the cognitive approach?
9. Is there homogamy in all relationships?
10. Has filter theory got cause and effect the wrong way round?
11. Does the rise of internet dating mean that filter theory is out of date?
12. Do opposites complement each other in a long-term relationship?
13. How does speed dating relate to filter theory?

Glossary

Key word	Definition
Bottleneck metaphor	The neck of a bottle helps to slow the flow of liquid as it narrows down the large mass into a smaller more manageable quantity.
Checks and balances	A system designed to ensure that no one person has complete control over all decisions.
Complementarity	A relationship in which different things improve or emphasise each other's qualities.
Face validity	When something 'looks like' it is a good measure, rather than having been tested.
Field of eligibles	All the people available for a person to have a relationship with.

Key word	Definition
Filter theory	An explanation of attraction in romantic relationships that stresses the role of filters in the formation, development and maintenance of relationships.
Heterogamy	A relationship formed between two people who are in some way different, particularly in terms of certain abilities/traits, e.g. one is organised but the other is able to stay calm under pressure.
Homogamy	A relationship formed between two people who are in some way culturally similar, e.g. age, social class, etc.
Similarity in attitudes	General agreement on a number of opinions.
Social demography	Social characteristics of a person such as their age, social class or geographic location.
Star-crossed lovers	People in a relationship that is doomed to fail because there are too many forces against it, e.g. non-matching astrological star signs.
Temporal validity	When something can be applied across different time periods, rather than just within the one it was tested in.

Plenary: Exam-style questions and answers with advisory comments

Question 1.

Explain what is meant by social demography in relation to the filter theory of romantic relationships? [2 marks]

Marks for this question: AO1 = 2

Advice: In a question like this, it's important to make sure you make it clear how this relates to psychology, so this will probably require an example. There is no need to provide any analysis or evaluation as both marks are for AO1: Knowledge and understanding.

Possible answer: Social demography refers to the social characteristics of people in the population such as age, ethnicity, religion or geographical location. It is the first filter identified by Kerckhoff and Davis in their filter theory and suggests that it is an important factor in attraction as it influences how people form relationships, e.g. you are more likely to get together with someone who lives near to you.

Question 2.

Describe and evaluate the filter theory as a factor in attraction in romantic relationships.   [16 marks]

Marks for this question: AO1 = 6 and AO3 = 10

Advice: This question is looking for both skills of knowledge and understanding and analysis and evaluation. As there are 6 marks for AO1 and 10 for AO3, there should be greater emphasis on the evaluation. However, all such extended writing questions are marked holistically and therefore it is important that the knowledge is accurate and detailed and that the evaluation is clear and effective.

Possible answer: The filter theory of romantic relationships was put forward by Kerckhoff and Davis and suggests that there is a series of filters that people use in the formation, development and maintenance of relationships and that these filters are important in our attraction to others. These filters allow us to narrow down from the field of eligibles (all of the people that we could form a relationship with) to just a few and, hopefully, in the end, just one.

The first filter is a social demographic one and this is based around the social characteristics of people, such as their age, ethnicity, religion and, importantly, their geographic location. The suggestion is that we are more likely to meet and form relationships with people who are demographically more like ourselves and, in the case of geographical location, live close enough for us to meet. According to Kerckhoff and Davis there is a tendency towards homogamy in relationships whereby people who are more socially or culturally similar come together.

The second filter is based around similarity in attitudes and focuses on the idea that once we have met someone and started to get to know them, we learn about their attitudes to and opinions on various topics. If we find that we tend to agree on certain values and opinions then we are more likely to continue in a relationship with that person, but if we find that we disagree completely, then it's unlikely that it will go any further, e.g. if one supports Wolves and the other supports West Brom!

The third filter seems quite different to the previous one as it suggests that it is what is different about people, rather than their similarities, that is important in the maintenance of relationships in the long term. This filter is about complementarity and argues that it is important that couples in a relationship have different skills that complement one another for relationships to last into the future. For example, if one partner is very organised, it would be useful if the other was very flexible, rather than them both having the same qualities, which might mean another skill is missing.

This theory seems to make a lot of sense and as such could be regarded as having strong face validity as it seems obvious that without social demographic features being in place, people are unlikely to meet or get together. However, it could be argued that this point is based around Western heterosexual relationships.

Lin et al. found in their study in Taiwan that while it is true that heterosexual and homosexual relationships are homogamous in terms of certain characteristics, this is not true of all characteristics. They found that, in terms of age and education, homosexual relationships were even more homogamous than heterosexual relationships, supporting filter theory; however they also found that homosexual relationships were more heterogamous in terms of family background, opposing filter theory. It seems as though the apparent validity of the theory may only relate to Western, heterosexual relationships, if it relates to any at all.

A further issue with the theory, in relation to similarity in attitudes at least, is the question of causation. Kerckhoff and Davis argue that it is similarity in attitudes that helps a relationship to develop, however, it may be that these attitudes only become similar as a result of being in a relationship and are therefore the effect of relationship development, rather than the cause of it.

Anderson et al. conducted a longitudinal study of young adults at the start of their relationship and then 6 months later, measuring their emotional responses through a series of discussions of sensitive topics that were either positive or negative. They found that there was an emotional convergence of responses over time, suggesting that the partners became more alike as the relationship developed. This questions filter theory as it makes it difficult to judge whether Kerckhoff and Davis were identifying a cause or an effect of relationship development and therefore questions the validity of their second filter.

Fortunately for Kerckhoff and Davis, there is some support for the complementarity filter in the maintenance of relationships, as Bohns et al. found in their study that having different skills had a positive effect on long-term relationships. Their findings were that when one partner in a couple was eagerly pressing ahead towards some goal that both partners desired, it was useful if the other partner was more vigilant and able to keep a check on things, so that in the end the whole process was more successful. It seems that without these opposite skills, the relationship would struggle, supporting the notion of complementarity in relationships.

One final point is that as filter theory was developed in the 1960s, it could be argued that it doesn't relate to the formation of relationships in the modern world, particularly with the advent of online dating and mobile dating apps like Tinder, and therefore it could be seen as lacking temporal validity. However, the internet has opened up the world to everyone and without the use of filters it's hard to imagine how that particular 'field of eligibles' could be narrowed down.

Mantell has argued that internet users are well versed in filtering and suggests that dating becomes like a military operation on these sites, not least due to the need to sort out the truth from the lies. Other researchers have found similar levels of filtering but argue that the main issue with this is checking that people actually look the way they claim, so it seems that physical attractiveness is the biggest issue, rather than the kind of filters identified by Kerckhoff and Davis.

References

Advtravlr, B.K. (2018) My first speed dating experience. *Nutty Talks*. 3 June 2018.
Anderson, C., Keltner, D. and John, O.P. (2003) Emotional convergence between people over time. *Journal of Personality and Social Psychology*, 84 (5): 1054.

Bohns, V.K., Lucas, G.M., Molden, D.C., Finkel, E.J., Coolsen, M.K., Kumashiro, M., Rusbult, C.E. and Higgins, E.T. (2013) Opposites fit: Regulatory focus complementarity and relationship well-being. *Social Cognition*, 31 (1): 1–14.

Couch, D. and Liamputtong, P. (2008) Online dating and mating: The use of the internet to meet sexual partners. *Qualitative Health Research*, 18 (2): 268–279.

Kerckhoff, A.C. and Davis, K.E. (1962) Value consensus and need complementarity in mate selection. *American Sociological Review*, 1 June: 295–303.

Lin, Z., Yu, W.H. and Su, K.H. (2019) Comparing same- and different-sex relationship dynamics: Experiences of young adults in Taiwan. *Demographic Research*, 40 (17): 431, 462. Published 5 March 2019. https://www. demographic-research.org/Volumes/Vol40/17.

Mantell, E.H. (2018) Searching for a partner on the internet and analogous decision-making problems. *Cogent Economics & Finance*, 6 (1).

Chapter 6
Theories of romantic relationships 1: Social exchange theory

Spec check

Theories of romantic relationships: social exchange theory

AO1 (Knowledge and understanding): Theories of romantic relationships: social exchange theory

The role of a **cost-benefit analysis** in the development of relationships

If you were in business and wanted to consider your level of success, you might take a look at your balance sheet, which would tell you about your assets and liabilities – in other words, how much you have coming in against how much you have going out. And you might regard your business as successful if you have more coming in than going out. This very unromantic proposition is the basic idea of Thibaut and Kelley's (1959) **social exchange theory**, which suggests that behaviour in a relationship is guided by this economic principle of increasing your rewards while lowering your costs, meaning that you will profit from the relationship in some way.

As everyone knows, relationships are hard work, and you need to feel like they are worth it. One way to judge this is through a cost-benefit analysis – how much am I putting in (costs) versus how much am I getting back (benefits). The costs of a relationship might be precious commodities, like how much time, effort and commitment you give to it, whereas the benefits might be other precious commodities like emotional support, praise and recognition, and sex. The exchange of these precious commodities will hopefully result in you feeling that you have gained more than you have lost and so you will feel satisfied in the relationship, but if you feel that you have lost more, then you will feel unsatisfied and considering dissolving the business, err sorry, relationship.

Think!

Does this reflect what real relationships are like?

How do you decide if a relationship is any good? What do you compare with?

How levels of comparison influence relationships

Unfortunately, the rewards and costs of a relationship aren't always as obvious as in a business and, as Blau (1964) argues, we can't really barter over them, e.g. 'If you won't love me, then I won't love you', so our judgement is somewhat more subjective and likely to be based around some form of comparison.

Comparison level

This is the simplest (and most subjective) form of comparison, as it suggests that we compare our actual relationship against our expectations for the relationship. If our relationship falls short of the profits we expect to get, then it's likely to be judged to be failing, but if they meet or exceed, then it can be judged to be a success.

Comparison level for alternatives

This is a slightly less subjective comparison as we are now comparing against other possible relationships that we could have. If we look around at the other possibilities and decide that one of them could be more profitable than our current relationship, then we are likely to go for it. Inevitably, this comparison is only likely to happen if there is a problem in the relationship, otherwise why would we be looking for other potential partners!

The stages of relationship development

According to the theory, the establishment and consolidation of rewards and costs in a relationship go through four stages:

1. *Sampling stage* – we find out how it works by observing what others do or by trying it out in our own relationships (romantic or otherwise), e.g. noticing that compliments lead to positive feedback.
2. *Bargaining stage* – at the start of a romantic relationship, we start to identify how much we are prepared to give and how much we expect back, e.g. compliments help to get what we want.
3. *Commitment stage* – having established how much we should be exchanging, the process now becomes more predictable, e.g. compliments are given and reciprocated on a regular basis.
4. *Institutionalisation stage* – rewards are now consolidated as the exchange has settled down into a recognisable pattern, e.g. compliments are given and reciprocated whenever something about our partner's appearance has changed.

What the stages do reflect is that most of the time, we are unable to objectively measure the benefits of a romantic relationship because they have become institutionalised and as such we don't notice them most of the time, especially because they are very subtle, but we still know they are there as we have seen them developing over a long period of time.

Mini plenary

Without referring back to the text, provide definitions of the following:

- **Cost-benefit analysis of relationships**
- **Comparison level**
- **Comparison level for alternatives**
- **Sampling stage**
- **Bargaining stage**
- **Commitment stage**
- **Institutionalisation stage**

AO2 (Application of knowledge): How does this apply in practice?

Interleave me now

Cost-benefit analysis and ethics

The decision to allow psychological research to go ahead is often considered by ethics committees who are able to judge the worth of a piece of research, at least partially, in terms of a cost-benefit analysis. They need to decide if the benefits of the research outweigh the possible costs to society. Possible costs of research might involve some form of damage to the participants themselves, to the reputation of psychology or science, or to certain groups in society in the case of socially sensitive research. The benefits could be some ground-breaking findings that change society forever – that could prove to make a big, positive change to society in some way.

Consequently, it's not an easy matter to simply say yes or no to some research as a balance needs to be considered between the costs and benefits and, ultimately, if one outweighs the other, then it will affect the decision in much the same way as we have considered for relationships. If the costs are too high and the benefits too low then, like our relationships, it could be the end of the road for the research

Think!

Are there any ethical issues arising from the social exchange theory of relationships?

Mini plenary

Bill and Ben have been in a relationship for 50 years and every Friday evening Ben buys Bill a bunch of flowers. Ben has never missed a week in 50 years and every Friday Bill gives Ben a big hug in return.

Using the material above, explain how social exchange theory would explain Bill's behaviour. Is there any other explanation for it?

AO3 (Analysis and evaluation of knowledge): How useful is this explanation?

Does the theory ignore equity?

One of the problems with social exchange theory is that it focuses heavily on an individual maximising their rewards, largely at the expense of the other partner. In reality, what most romantic partners are looking for is some form of reciprocation and fairness. Equity theory (Chapter 7) argues that as long as there is a degree of fairness in relation to what each partner is giving to the relationship then it's fine, so it could be argued that social exchange theory has failed to take account of this important distinction. This might explain why there is very little research supporting the notion that one partner is seeking to gain *more* than the other from the relationship.

However, Kelley and Thibaut (1978) did extend their theory to include a greater role for interdependence and a recognition that each partner must provide the other with something, so rather than seeing the relationship as a contest for who can get the most, interdependence suggests that both should benefit and, more importantly, feel that they have benefitted, to some degree or other equally, even though the value of what each person is putting in may not be equal. This extension of the theory does seem to make it more reasonable and rational than it was in its original form.

Is there evidence for the comparison levels?

In spite of the shortcomings of the theory mentioned above, there has been some research support for the comparison levels identified by Thibaut and Kelley, particularly in relation to the idea that satisfaction in a relationship comes when the perceived levels of rewards meet expectations, as identified in Thibaut and Kelley's comparison levels.

For the purposes of her study, Dainton (2000) looked at maintenance behaviours such as positivity, openness, assurances, social networks and sharing tasks as behaviours that have been shown to lead to greater satisfaction in a relationship. She found that there was a moderately significant correlation between expectations of this kind of behaviour being fulfilled and relationship satisfaction, such that the more an individual perceived his/her partner as using maintenance behaviour relative to his/her own expectations, the more satisfied the individual was with the relationship.

This provides some support for the comparison levels identified by Thibaut and Kelley as it seems to fit with the idea that if your expectations are fulfilled then you are satisfied with the relationship. However, Dainton did go on to argue that she had only found moderate support and that this comparison effect was probably not a useful measure on its own.

Is the theory relevant to romantic relationships at all?

One of the problems with social exchange theory is that it just doesn't seem very romantic, so at a face validity level, it doesn't seem to make good sense. This issue has been supported by Clark and Mills (2011), who have argued that when looking at relationships it's necessary to distinguish between exchange relationships that are based on the kinds of exchange that are identified by this theory and communal relationships that are not.

From their point of view, exchange relationships are ones in which you would expect at least a comparable benefit being returned for any benefit that has been given out, but these relationships are the sort you might have at work, not romantic relationships. However, communal relationships, which are the romantic type, have no such expectations of receiving a comparable reward. In fact, benefits would often be given out in communal relationships with no expectation of receiving anything back, just to support the other person's welfare.

Therefore, it seems as though the whole basis of the social exchange theory has been undermined by this, and that an overly economic approach to relationships not only lacks face validity, but also lacks support from research.

How can we measure the costs and benefits of behaviour?

A further problem for the economic basis of social exchange theory comes from the difficulty of assigning values to human behaviour. If you are involved in the trade of materials then the value is based on factors that are largely determined by the market and are, to some extent or other, objective. However, when dealing with human behaviour, particularly in a 'loving' context in which people are doing things for one another, it's not so easy.

Earlier, Dainton identified maintenance behaviour as the sort of thing that couples do for one another in a romantic relationship, such as positivity, which she went on to identify as behaving in a cheerful and optimistic manner – something that is clearly difficult to put a value on. She also identified assurances such as messages stressing commitment to the relationship ('You know I love you', etc.), which might be measurable (e.g. I said it twice and you only said it once) but are largely subjective.

Consequently, it is difficult to make judgements about costs and benefits when you are dealing with something that has no objective value and this, therefore, again makes it difficult to apply to romantic relationships. However, sometimes couples do try to value each other's contribution, particularly when it comes to one of the other things identified by Dainton, sharing tasks. Couples will sometimes compare each other's contribution to tasks, e.g. mowing the lawn versus cleaning the toilet, however, when this happens it is usually a symptom of an already failing relationship, rather than the cause of it.

Think!

If you wanted to study the costs and benefits of exchanges in a romantic relationship, how would you go about it? Would you use quantitative or qualitative methods? Would you try to get the feelings of the individual? Would that be worthwhile?

Mini plenary

Using the evaluation points above and the thoughts about studying behaviour that you have just developed, write a short piece of about 250 words to explain the problems you would have in investigating the impact of social exchange theory on romantic relationships. Consider both the practical and theoretical problems.

A modern issue – would you have a prenup?

It's time to talk about the 'P word': prenup. Short for prenuptial agreement, a prenup is a legally binding contract two people sign before marrying that covers financial issues and the future of assets in the event of a divorce. Because of its delicate nature, prenup has long been a dirty word with couples. However, prenups might slowly be shedding their stigma.

New research

BUSINESS INSIDER

Prenups aren't just for the rich or famous – more millennials are signing them before getting married, and you probably should too

Hillary Hoffower

5 February 2019, 1.45 pm

According to the American Academy of Matrimonial Lawyers, the number of prenuptial agreements is increasing, particularly among millennials. Data from the lawyers surveyed for this research shows that most saw a rise in prenups among this group between 2013 and 2016.

One of the factors involved here is age of marriage, the US census shows that the median age at which men and women get married has gone up from 27 to 29.9 for men and from 25.5 to 28 for women. It seems that the longer they take to get married, the more likely they are to accrue wealth that needs protection. This is particularly true for females who have become more independently wealthy than their mothers were.

'The role of women in relationships and family structures is shifting,' Theresa Viera, family law attorney at Sodoma Law, said. '… With women attaining college degrees at higher rates, accessing higher wages than ever before, and single women purchasing homes more often than single men, we may be seeing the effect of female millennials who want to protect their financial interests when entering into marriage.'

However, it isn't just assets that millennials are trying to protect, they are also trying to protect themselves from their partner's debts – something that has become a real issue for this group, with increasingly high levels of student debt. Debts from student loans appear to have become such an issue that 10 per cent of those with them blame their divorce on it, according to a report by Student Loan Hero.

Question time

What does this suggest about the importance of social exchange in romantic relationships?

Are prenups unromantic? Would you have one?

How would you respond if your prospective spouse were to ask for one? Would it be the end?

1. What is the role of a cost-benefit analysis in relationships?
2. What is meant by comparison level in relationships?
3. What is meant by comparison level for alternatives in relationships?
4. What are the four stages of development in relationships?
5. What is involved in a cost-benefit analysis in ethics?
6. Are there any ethical issues in social exchange theory?
7. Does social exchange theory ignore equity?
8. Is there any evidence for social exchange theory?
9. Is the theory relevant to romantic relationships at all?
10. Is it possible to put a value on romantic behaviour?
11. What do prenuptial agreements tell us about social exchange theory?

Glossary

Key word	Definition
Comparison level	Refers to the expectations for the relationship based on past experience or the perceived norm.
Comparison level for alternatives	The idea that people are satisfied in their relationships based on their extent to which they perceive their ability to exchange their current relationship for a better one.
Cost-benefit analysis	A way of making decisions that compares the likely financial loss of an action against the likely financial gain.
Face validity	When something 'looks like' it is a good measure, rather than having been tested.
Institutionalised	Become established as a norm in an organisation or culture.
Interdependence	Focuses on two people providing benefits for one another that help them achieve a goal, even if they aren't considered equal value.
Precious commodities	Useful or valuable items that are usually bought and sold, e.g. oil.

Plenary: Exam-style questions and answers with advisory comments

Question 1.

Explain what is meant by the term social exchange in relation to romantic relationships? [2 marks]

Marks for this question: AO1 = 2

Advice: In a question like this, it's important to make sure you are making it clear how this relates to psychology, so this will probably require an example. There is no need to provide any analysis or evaluation as both marks are for AO1: Knowledge and understanding.

Possible answer: Social exchange is an economic explanation for the development and maintenance of relationships that focuses on the need to maximise your rewards or benefits and minimise your costs. A person will be satisfied in the relationship if they can get more out than they put in, e.g. taking a little time to pay a compliment but getting a lot of praise and recognition for it.

Question 2.

Describe and evaluate the social exchange theory of romantic relationships. [16 marks]

Marks for this question: AO1 = 6 and AO3 = 10

Advice: This question is looking for both skills of knowledge and understanding and analysis and evaluation. As there are 6 marks for AO1 and 10 for AO3, there should be greater emphasis on the evaluation. However, all such extended writing questions are marked holistically and therefore it is important that the knowledge is accurate and detailed and that the evaluation is clear and effective.

Possible answer: Social exchange theory focuses on the economic implications of romantic relationships and suggests that behaviour in relationships is motivated by a cost-benefit analysis in that we are trying to minimise the cost of our behaviour and maximise the benefit or reward we get for it. Relationships can have many costs, such as time, effort and commitment, but can also have benefits, such as affection and recognition.

One way of identifying the costs and benefits is to compare the relationship at two levels identified by Thibaut and Kelley who came up with this theory. The first level is the comparison level, which involves comparing your current relationship against your expectations for what you think you should be getting out of a relationship. This comparison is likely to be based on past experience of your own relationships or what you have observed from the social norm for your culture, e.g. in the media. The second level is the comparison level for alternatives, which involves comparing your current relationship against potential alternatives, and if you decide that the alternatives can offer more benefits then you are likely to be dissatisfied, if not then you're okay.

Thibaut and Kelley have also identified four stages that people go through in the development of a relationship, which are all focused on the issue of costs and benefits. The first stage is *sampling* where we find out how to gain rewards at minimal cost by trying it out in our own relationships, romantic or otherwise, which then helps out in the early stages of romantic relationships as we start *bargaining* (second stage) with our partner to ensure that we set the boundaries for what we are prepared to give and what we expect back. As our commitment (third stage) develops, the costs and benefits become more predictable, until finally the process becomes institutionalised (fourth stage) as we have a set pattern of costs and benefits.

If this doesn't sound very romantic, that's probably because it isn't and one of the arguments that is made against the theory is that it's more relevant to work relationships than romantic ones.

Clark and Mills have argued that the theory is more relevant to exchange relationships, which are the sort that we have with our work colleagues, than communal relationships, which are the sort that we have with our romantic partners. In the latter, we are likely to do things for our partner with little or sometimes no expectation of getting anything back, simply because we are concerned about their welfare.

A further problem with the theory is that it doesn't take account of the need for fairness in relationships, equity theory argues that most people in a relationship are happy to do things for their partner as long as they get something back that is fair and reasonable. However, Thibaut and Kelley did change their theory later to include the notion of interdependence, which suggests that the relationship is less of a contest for who can get the most and more of a recognition that both can give something, even if what each can give is different and may not be of equal value.

On the question of the value of what each partner can give to a relationship, a further problem with attempting to value the contribution of each partner in a relationship is that most of the things we are talking about in a romantic relationship can't be quantified. Unlike economic transactions in business, things like affection and emotional support are not quantifiable and often only have value in terms of the situation in which they occur. Whether something is valuable or not to a relationship is very subjective and therefore impossible to objectively measure in the way this theory suggests.

However, there is some empirical support for some parts of the theory. Dainton wanted to find out if the comparison levels identified by the theory were relevant to real relationships. They questioned people about how their partner meeting their expectations for the kind of affectionate and emotionally supportive behaviour mentioned above affects their satisfaction with the relationship. They found that there was a moderately significant correlation between the two, which seems to support the idea of the comparison levels.

Furthermore, there is evidence that young people entering into a relationship are considering financial issues as, according to the American Academy of Matrimonial Lawyers, the use of prenuptial agreements is increasing, which suggests that we are trying to minimise the potential costs that could come from relationships.

References

Blau, P.M. (1964) *Exchange and Power in Social Life*. New York: John Wiley & Sons.

Clark, M.S. and Mills, J.R. (2011) A theory of communal (and exchange) relationships. In: P.A.M. Van Lange, A.W. Kruglanski and E.T. Higgins (eds), *Handbook of Theories of Social Psychology*, Vol. 2. London and Thousand Oaks, CA: Sage, pp. 232–250.

Dainton, M. (2000) Maintenance behaviors, expectations for maintenance, and satisfaction: Linking comparison levels to relational maintenance strategies. *Journal of Social and Personal Relationships*, 17 (6): 827–842.

Hoffower, H. (2019) Prenups aren't just for the rich or famous – more millennials are signing them before getting married, and you probably should too. *Business Insider*, 4 February.

Kelley, H.H. and Thibaut, J.W. (1978) *Interpersonal Relations: A Theory of Interdependence*. New York: John Wiley & Sons.

Thibaut, J.W. and Kelley, H.H. (1959) *The Social Psychology of Groups*. New York: John Wiley & Sons.

Chapter 7
Theories of romantic relationships 2: Equity theory

Spec check

Theories of romantic relationships: equity theory

AO1 (Knowledge and understanding): Theories of romantic relationships: equity theory

The role of equity in relationships

Some would say that a good relationship is all about give and take, if you want to get something out of it, then you have to be prepared to give something back. Unlike social exchange theory, which is all about what you can get out of a relationship, equity theory is about being prepared to give as much as you get, because that's the right thing to do.

In this extension of social exchange theory, the most important consideration is fairness, according to Walster et al. (1978), as long as both partners in a relationship consider the inputs (what they put in) and outcomes (what they get out) of the relationship to be fairly distributed then that's fine, however if one seems to be over-benefitting then this will cause dissatisfaction. Naturally, this will mostly be on the part of the one who is under-benefitting as they will feel anger and resentment but the over-benefitting one is also likely to feel dissatisfied as they may feel guilt and anxiety.

The difference between equity and equality

Equity theory proposes that the distribution of inputs and outputs is both relative and subjective, so the contribution of each partner doesn't have to be exactly the same. One person may have a job that requires them to work long hours and be out of the house all day; the other may have to be in the house for most of the day, doing other forms of work; and, as long as each partner regards it as fair and reasonable, then that's fine. For example, if one partner spends a lot of time organising events and activities that both can do together, they will both benefit from this without the other partner doing much of the work. However, if the second partner provides more affection and emotional support than the other, then again they will both benefit without the second partner doing much work. The important thing is that they both recognise not just what the other partner does, but also what they get out of it as being relatively fair (not necessarily equal). They do not have to do the same things nor do they each have to have exactly equal value, but they do have to be recognised as comparable, otherwise dissatisfaction will occur and the relationship will be judged to be inequitable.

The consequences of inequity

The main consequence of inequity is distress as partners in an inequitable relationship have the kinds of feelings outlined above (anger or guilt), which then lead to dissatisfaction and feeling uncomfortable with the relationship. The theory predicts that there will be a strong correlation between inequity and feeling uncomfortable in a relationship, such that the more inequity in a relationship, the more uncomfortable partners feel.

The theory proposes that partners in inequitable relationships will do all that they can to attempt to restore equity by redressing the balance of inputs and outcomes. There are different ways of doing this but the simplest way would be to attempt to alter the input of one or other of them so that the over-benefitting partner is putting more in and the under-benefitting partner is putting less in. Naturally, there is more incentive on the part of the under-benefitting partner to change things but as the over-benefitting partner is also distressed, they should still feel motivated to change.

Think!

If you were in a relationship and you could see that your partner was feeling distressed and uncomfortable, how would it make you feel?

If there was something you could do about it, would you do it, even if it meant more work for you?

Mini plenary

Use the words provided to complete the paragraph describing equity theory:

outcomes   benefitting   equal   distress   fair   equity   benefitting inputs

Equity theory suggests that in a relationship people need to feel that their contribution is .... and therefore, that the balance between their .... and .... is reasonable in comparison to their partner. Each partner doesn't have to make an .... contribution, just as long as it seems right to both in their judgement. If the relationship is inequitable, then both partners will suffer ...., which will lead to dissatisfaction with the relationship. Both the over- .... partner and the under- .... partner will feel the need to restore .... and this should create satisfaction with the relationship again.

AO2 (Application of knowledge): How does this apply in practice?

Interleave mc now

Gender bias and relationships

Bias arises in psychological research when one group or individual is treated differently and often more favourably than another.

There has been a tendency in psychological research to favour men at the expense or women. This has at least partly come about due to the gender-biased nature of society, but, let's face it, that's no excuse. One area where this bias is likely to appear is in the study of intimate heterosexual relationships.

Forms of gender bias

Androcentrism is the tendency to focus attention on males at the expense of females.

Alpha bias is one that tends to overplay the importance of gender in our understanding of human behaviour and suggests that men and women are completely different; and, either implicitly or, sometimes, explicitly suggests that the behaviour of the two should be explained quite differently.

Beta bias is one that tends to downplay the importance of gender in our understanding of human behaviour and tends to suggest that we can ignore the issue of gender as men and women are basically the same.

Gender-role stereotyping and the perception of equity

One of the things that becomes clear when looking at equity in a relationship is that a lot of people's feelings about it come from their subjective perception of how fair is their relationship. Such subjective judgements are fine as long as we can assume that they are made equally, without the influence of other social factors. Unfortunately, this is impossible as none of these judgements is made in a vacuum and so we must also consider the effect of other social pressures.

One such pressure is gender-role stereotyping and how people judge their own contribution to a relationship based on this. If you judge your contribution based on what is traditionally expected of men and women in a relationship, then you may come to the conclusion that it's fair as you are not expecting it to be different, if you don't then you may come to a very different conclusion.

Donaghue and Fallon (2003) compared the level of gender-role self-stereotyping of men and women in long-term relationships and found that those with a high level, making them more traditional in their view of gender-role stereotypes, had a different view of the importance of equity than did those with a low level who were less traditional. The high-level group tended to compare their relationship to the norm for others in same-sex relationships, whereas the low-level group tended to use equity as a judgement of their satisfaction.

Unfortunately, ignoring the impact of gender-role stereotyping seems to indicate a form of beta bias in equity theory and research, such that it's hard to apply the theory to both men and women without understanding how their perceptions are affected by it.

Question time

What might the effect of gender-role stereotypes be on your perception of equity in a relationship?

Is it possible to incorporate this into research so as to avoid beta bias?

Mini plenary

Sal and Gerry have been together for 15 years and are generally happy but recently Sal has started to notice that Gerry isn't really bringing much to their relationship, Gerry will go straight out into the garden after getting home from work, will often ignore Sal and spend the rest of the night on social media on the mobile phone. Sal is left to get on with everything in the house while still holding down a full-time job.

What would equity theory say about the likely prospects for Sal and Gerry's relationship? What could they do to make it better?

AO3 (Analysis and evaluation of knowledge): How useful is this explanation?

Is over-benefitting as bad as under-benefitting?

One of the more questionable aspects of the theory is the claim that over-benefitting leads to dissatisfaction, as this seems to go against common sense – it may be that partners in this situation would be quite happy to continue in such a way.

An experimental study by Sprecher (2018) involved 'priming' participants to write about past equitable/inequitable relationships and then seeing the effect on their self-reported satisfaction. Sprecher found significantly higher levels of reported stress and dissatisfaction in inequitable relationships than equitable ones. However, she did not find a significant difference between under-benefitting and over-benefitting, even though the distress scores were slightly higher and the satisfaction scores slightly lower for under-benefitting than for over-benefitting.

Overall, these findings do provide some support for equity theory and they have done so in a way that is not simply correlational or longitudinal, thus showing a causal relationship between both forms of inequity and relationship distress and dissatisfaction. This is particularly significant as the participants were not being asked about artificial scenarios, which increases its validity.

However, this is still retrospective data as it's based on the participant's recollection of how they felt at some point in the past, which is not the same as having the experience at the time. This may cause the results to be distorted as feelings now may be different from feelings at the time, and this does bring the validity of the study into question.

Is there a problem with causation?

A further issue that raises questions about the usefulness of equity theory is whether the relationship between equity and satisfaction is the right way round. The theory is suggesting that equity leads to satisfaction but it could be that satisfaction in a relationship encourages partners to act in a more equitable manner in their relationship.

Sprecher (2001) conducted a longitudinal study of 101 dating couples recruited through university newspaper advertisements and posters placed around the university campus in a Midwestern university in America. The participants completed questionnaires at different points over the course of five years to assess the importance of equity in relation to satisfaction in their relationships.

She found some evidence that under-benefitting (but not over-benefitting) was associated with relationship dissatisfaction and break-up, however more evidence was found for the reverse causal direction in that satisfaction contributed to a decrease in under-benefitting inequity. It seems that as commitment and investment increase in a relationship, and people become more satisfied, they behave in ways that are increasingly equitable. Furthermore, if relationship satisfaction goes down, partners are more likely to notice the inequity in their relationship, which also suggests that the cause is the other way round from what the theory suggests.

Sprecher argues that rewards are more important than equity and that 'comparison for alternatives', in line with social exchange theory, plays a part in relationships, but again only when people have already become dissatisfied. She makes the point that, if there is an issue with equity, it is likely to come to light when a relationship is started (which she didn't look at), meaning that the couple will not go on to form a long-term relationship – which might explain why she found a lack of influence for it. She also recognises that her study was conducted purely with heterosexual couples, and with mostly white students, so it may not be representative of homosexual couples and those from other cultures.

Are there cultural differences in the effect of inequity?

One of the problems with a lot of the research supporting equity theory is that it is based around an analysis of individualistic cultures and not so much on collectivistic cultures. This may mean that the theory suffers from cultural bias.

In order to address this problem, Aumer-Ryan et al. (2007) compared the effect of equity on satisfaction in relationships across two different cultures, one in the USA with 300 students (207 women and 93 men) from the University of Hawaii (considered to be an individualistic culture) and the other in the West Indies with 122 students (108 women and 14 men) from the University of the West Indies in Jamaica (considered to be a collectivistic culture). The students were surveyed on how equitable their relationship was, how important they considered equity to be and how satisfied they were with their relationship.

The findings of the survey were that both cultures considered equity to be very important in a relationship – which supports equity theory. However, the Americans regarded their relationships as more equitable and satisfying than the West Indians and, importantly, while the Americans found their relationships to be more satisfying when they were equitable, the West Indians found their relationships to be more satisfying when they were over-benefitting. This clearly goes against the theory and suggests that there are cultural differences in the effects of equity on relationship satisfaction.

The researchers suggested that it may be due to the different family structures in the two types of culture, with the West Indian family being more tightly knit and the fact that West Indians rely a lot more on their extended families (parents, grandparents, etc.) for emotional and practical support. However, there were a lot more women from both cultures taking part in the study, particularly for the West Indies study, so it may be that the study is not truly representative of both genders.

Are individual differences important in the effect of equity?

One of the issues with equity theory is that it assumes that everyone has the same need for equity in their relationship, when it might be that there are individual differences and some people may not need to have it.

Huseman et al. (1987) proposed that although people do act and react in a consistent manner, these actions and reactions are individually different, such that people are different in their sensitivity to equity. They identified three 'types' of people: equity sensitive people, who fit with the theory as they like to have equity in their relationships; benevolents, who are happy to give more than they get from a relationship; and entitleds, who like to get more than they give to a relationship.

They believe that this is a personality trait that develops partly due to the influence of culture (e.g. religious heritage) and partly due to their inherent personality being one that is more empathetic. This suggests that equity theory is too simplistic in its description of relationships as it lacks the sophistication needed to explain all of the different types of personality that make up a relationship. It is quite easy to see how this equity sensitivity model could apply to relationship satisfaction: as long as a benevolent type forms a relationship with an entitled type, both should be happy and satisfied.

Question time

Does the evidence suggest that equity is important to everyone?

What other features of a relationship are important?

Is it possible to say that one is more important than another?

Using the evaluation points above, try to evaluate the following statement.

Satisfaction in a relationship is built around equity.

Arguments for	Arguments against

A modern issue – can changing your perception of equity make your relationship better?

The need for equity may be important in a relationship but part of our judgement of equity may be related to how much we expect from our partner and it could be that altering our expectations for our partner's contribution to the relationship will help even more.

New research

Psychology Today

An effortless relationship hack

Improve your romantic relationship in one easy way, no time or effort required

Madeleine A. Fugère

Posted 23 December 2017

In this article, the author explains how upon arriving home one day last week, she found that her husband had washed all of the dishes, which is remarkable enough and should have been cause for joy, except that he had not cleaned the left-over food from the drain, which infuriated her. Her initial anger and frustration turned to happiness and gratitude once she realised that she was looking at this the wrong way and should have been focusing on what he had done, rather than what he hadn't. This made her think about how just changing her perception of the situation could change her feelings and how this might broaden out into other areas of their relationship.

Change your perceptions

This story is closely related to equity theory, developed by John Stacey Adams in 1965. Adams argued that relationship satisfaction is related to our perception of the costs and benefits we get from our relationships and the amount of investment that we make in them.

According to Adams, when we feel as though we are putting in more than we are getting out then we become dissatisfied. Consequently, we could change how much we are putting in or we could simply change our perception of that and, rather than just focus on our own contribution, think a little bit more about the contribution our partner is making. This is likely to be a lot easier as changing our thoughts is a lot easier than changing our behaviours. Grote and Clark (2001) point out that 'although we are almost always aware of our own contributions to the relationship (I always notice when I do the laundry), we may not always be aware of our partner's contributions'.

Conclusion

If you use this relatively effortless strategy, it's possible that it could lead to a much happier, more satisfactory relationship.

Question time

What does this suggest about equity theory as a factor in romantic relationships? Based on the strategy outlined above, does it sound like a 'good option' for the people who are looking for a satisfactory relationship or is it just a case of 'fooling yourself' to make it seem like everything's okay?

Chapter plenary

1. What is meant by equity in romantic relationships?
2. What is the difference between equity and equality in relationships?
3. What are the consequences of inequity in relationships?
4. What can partners do to restore equity to their relationship?
5. How does gender bias apply to relationships?
6. What's the effect of gender-role stereotyping on the perception of equity in a relationship?
7. What evidence is there to suggest beta bias in equity theory and research?
8. Is over-benefitting as bad as under-benefitting?
9. Is there a problem of causation in equity theory?
10. Are there cultural differences in the importance of equity in relationships?
11. Are there individual differences in the importance of equity in relationships?
12. Can changing your perception of equity make your relationship better?

Key word	Definition
Alpha bias	The tendency to overplay the importance of gender in our understanding of human behaviour; suggests that men and women are completely different and either implicitly or, sometimes, explicitly suggests that the behaviour of the two should be explained quite differently.
Androcentric	The tendency to focus attention on males at the expense of females.
Benevolents	Individuals who want to have an unfair balance of inputs and outcomes in a relationship in their partner's favour.
Beta bias	The tendency to downplay the importance of gender in our understanding of human behaviour; suggests that men and women are the same and that the behaviour of the two should be explained identically.
Bias	One group or individual is treated differently, and often more favourably, than another.
Collectivistic cultures	Societies that are based on collective achievement and the common good.
Comparison for alternatives	The idea that people are satisfied in their relationships based on their extent to which they perceive their ability to exchange their current relationship for a better one.
Empathetic	Being in touch with other people's feelings.
Entitleds	Individuals who want to have an unfair balance of inputs and outcomes in a relationship in their own favour.
Equality	The balance between what you put in and get out being exactly the same, rather than just fairly distributed, which is equity.
Equity sensitive	Individuals who want to have a fair balance of inputs and outcomes in their relationship.
Equity theory	A theory of relationships that suggests that fairness is important for a satisfying relationship.
Gender-role self-stereotyping	Your own beliefs about your gender role conform to the traditional/common beliefs about it.
Individualistic cultures	Societies that are based on individual achievement and personal gain.
Inequity	What is put in and taken out by each partner isn't fairly distributed.
Inputs and outcomes	The balance between how much you give to a relationship compared to how much you get out.

Key word	Definition
Over-benefitting	Getting significantly more out of a relationship than you put in.
Priming	A technique used in some experiments to provide people with a stimulus that gets them thinking about a particular topic, which they can then be tested on.
Retrospective data	Information that has been gathered about events that happened at some time in the past and may be difficult to accurately recall now.
Social exchange theory	A theory that suggests that people in a relationship attempt to minimise costs and maximise benefits.
Under-benefitting	Getting significantly less out of a relationship than you put in.

Plenary: Exam-style questions and answers with advisory comments

Question 1.

Explain what is meant by the term equity in relation to romantic relationships? [2 marks]

Marks for this question: AO1 = 2

Advice: In a question like this, it's important to make sure you are making it clear how this relates to psychology, so it will probably require an example. There is no need to provide any analysis or evaluation as both marks are for AO1: Knowledge and understanding.

Possible answer: Equity in romantic relationships refers to fairness in the distribution of what each partner puts in and gets out of a relationship. How much each partner puts in and gets out doesn't have to be exactly equal, it just needs to be seen to be fair. For example, one may spend a lot of time organising events while the other spends a lot of time giving emotional support, this seems fair because they both give time to it even though it doesn't need to be exactly the same amount of time.

Question 2.

Describe and evaluate the equity theory of romantic relationships. [16 marks]

Marks for this question: AO1 = 6 and AO3 = 10

Advice: This question is looking for both skills of knowledge and understanding and analysis and evaluation. As there are 6 marks for AO1 and 10 for AO3, there should be greater emphasis on the evaluation. However, all such extended writing questions are marked holistically and therefore it is important that the knowledge is accurate and detailed and that the evaluation is clear and effective.

Possible answer: Unlike social exchange theory, equity theory focuses on the need to achieve fairness in the distribution of costs and benefits in a relationship. According to Walster et al. as long as both partners consider what each is putting in and getting out of a relationship is fair then the relationship will be regarded as satisfying. If the distribution of inputs and outcomes is unfairly balanced so that one over-benefits or under-benefits, then the relationship will be regarded as unsatisfactory and may break up.

Both over-benefitting and under-benefitting can lead to distress as the over-benefitting partner will feel guilt and the under-benefitting partner will feel resentment. The distress caused by inequity will cause both partners to feel dissatisfied and uncomfortable in the relationship and the theory predicts that the more inequity there is in a relationship the more uncomfortable both partners will feel.

It's important to recognise that equity is not the same as equality and that partners in a relationship don't need to be doing exactly the same or giving or taking exactly the same amount as each other, as long as each partner perceives the distribution of inputs and outcomes to be fair. So, if one partner provides a lot of emotional support and the other doesn't, that's fine as long as the other partner makes a contribution in some other way, for example by organising events for them both to take part in.

If a relationship is inequitable and causing distress or dissatisfaction, then both partners are likely to try to restore equity by redressing the balance between inputs and outcomes. One way to do this is by the under-benefitting partner putting in slightly less and hopefully this would encourage the over-benefitting partner to put in slightly more so that equity can be restored.

One of the issues with this theory concerns the extent to which over-benefitting partners are seen to be suffering in a situation where they are taking more and giving less to a relationship. It's not clear whether they would have the same incentive to change things as their under-benefitting partner.

Sprecher tested the effect of both forms of inequity using an experimental technique in which participants were primed to feel certain emotions by being asked to describe a relationship in which they had over- or under-benefitted and they were then asked questions about their level of satisfaction with the situation. She found significantly higher levels of stress and dissatisfaction in inequitable relationships than equitable ones but only found a slight difference between over-benefitting and under-benefitting, suggesting that the theory is correct in the belief that over-benefitting is as bad, or nearly as bad, as under-benefitting.

However, although the study didn't use artificial scenarios, which increases its validity, it was still reliant on retrospective data that may cause the recall of the details and feelings of these events to be distorted and therefore less valid.

Although the study above was experimental and therefore could potentially show cause and effect, most of the evidence for this theory is correlational and may find it difficult to show causation. A further problem with this is that it may be getting the relationship between equity and dissatisfaction the wrong way round. Another study conducted by Sprecher found very little evidence for the idea that inequity causes dissatisfaction but did find stronger evidence for the idea that dissatisfaction causes inequity.

This finding could be explained by the fact that once people start to feel dissatisfied in their relationship, they then also begin to notice inequity in their relationship; or you could say that if they feel satisfied in their relationship, they work harder to make it more equitable as they feel greater empathy for their partner.

One of the problems with the Sprecher study outlined above is that it was conducted with white university students and therefore could be accused of cultural bias, as it fails to examine the potential differences between cultures. This potential difference was studied by Aumer-Ryan et al. by comparing the effect of equity on relationships between US students who live in an individualistic culture and West Indian students who live in a collectivistic culture.

The main finding of this study was that US students expressed higher levels of satisfaction when they were involved in an equitable relationship, but their West Indian counterparts were more satisfied in relationships when they were over-benefitting, suggesting that the theory doesn't adequately account for cultural differences and is therefore only applicable to individualistic cultures.

Further problems in considering differences between certain groups arise with the possible gender bias of this theory. As the theory is mostly about the perception of fairness in relationships, it could be that due to gender-role stereotypes in society, women and men may have different views on what is and is not a fair balance of inputs and outcomes. Donaghue and Fallon found that people who have less traditional gender-role views tend to believe in the importance of equity in relationships, but those with more traditional gender-role views tend to look to the society norm for their view. This may mean that women are being encouraged to accept that they should give more, and still feel satisfied, than their male partners – and that judging relationship satisfaction in this way ignores the real differences between the positions of men and women in society and so could be accused of beta bias.

References

Adams, J.S. (1965) Inequity in social exchange. *Advances in Experimental Social Psychology*, 2: 267–299.

Aumer-Ryan, K., Hatfield, E.C. and Frey, R. (2007) Examining equity theory across cultures. *Interpersonal: An International Journal on Personal Relationships*, 1 (1): 61–75.

Donaghue, N. and Fallon, B.J. (2003) Gender-role self-stereotyping and the relationship between equity and satisfaction in close relationships. *Sex Roles*, 48 (5–6): 217–230.

Fugère, M.A. (2017) Four effortless relationship hacks – Improve your romantic relationship in four easy ways, no time or effort required. *Psychology Today*, 23 December 2017.

Grote, N. and Clark, M. (2001) Perceiving unfairness in the family: Cause or consequence of marital distress? *Journal of Personality and Social Psychology*, 80 (2): 281–293.

Huseman, R.C., Hatfield, J.D. and Miles, E.W. (1987) A new perspective on equity theory: The equity sensitivity construct. *Academy of Management Review*, 12 (2): 222–234.

Sprecher, S. (2018) Inequity leads to distress and a reduction in satisfaction: Evidence from a priming experiment. *Journal of Family Issues*, 39 (1): 230–244.

Walster, E., Walster, G.W. and Berscheid, E. (1978) *Equity: Theory and Research*. Boston, MA: Allyn and Bacon.

Chapter 8
Theories of romantic relationships 3: Rusbult's investment model

Spec check

Theories of romantic relationships: Rusbult's investment model of commitment, satisfaction, comparison with alternatives and investment

AO1 (Knowledge and understanding): Theories of romantic relationships

The role of investment in relationships

The investment model is not so much a theory of how people *get together* in a relationship but of how people *stay together*. The issue of investment, like most of the other theories looked at so far, is borrowed from business studies to look at how investing in something creates a level of commitment that is hard to break. The theory is developed from the kind of interdependence put forward by Thibaut and Kelley in the later version of their theory but this theory is more to do with dependence and how we become dependent on a relationship (see Chapter 6). Commitment is a very important part of the theory, as it allows us to understand how people become tied to a relationship due to the level of commitment that they have put in. If you have invested a lot into a relationship, it will become quite difficult to leave. According to Rusbult et al. (2011), commitment is the most important factor in relationships and is influenced by three factors that help to explain how people become so committed to their relationship: satisfaction, comparison with alternatives and investment size.

The influence of satisfaction, comparison with alternatives and investment size

Satisfaction

As we have already seen, satisfaction is important in understanding people's relationships and it is of particular importance in this model. Satisfaction relates to the kind of costs and benefits identified by Thibaut and Kelley, such that if the costs of a relationship are low and the benefits are high, then the relationship is likely to be satisfying. However, this alone is not enough to explain why people stay in relationships because, if it were, then people would just leave when the costs are too high and the benefits too low. Consequently, there must be other factors that commit people to a relationship.

Comparison with alternatives

In order to decide whether you should stay in a relationship or not, you might decide to consider the possible alternatives. If there are a number of alternatives that you could pursue then you are likely to consider leaving. However, further analysis of these alternatives is required to consider whether or not they are more beneficial and less costly than your current relationship. If not, then you are likely to stick with your current relationship.

Investment size

This third factor is clearly crucial in determining commitment. As has already been said, the level of investment in an enterprise is likely to make you think very hard about the extent to which you are prepared to give up on your investment. Any investment in a relationship comes at a potential cost and the higher the investment, the greater the potential cost if you decide to pull out. According to Rusbult (1980), investments may be of two sorts, intrinsic investments, which include resources that are closely tied to the relationship such as time, money, energy and emotion, and extrinsic investments, which arise out of that, such as a house, car, children and mutual friends, which would all be lost if the relationship ended.

These three factors combine to produce commitment to a relationship, so that a high level of satisfaction combined with less desirable alternatives and a significant amount of investment produce a high level of commitment that makes it hard to simply give up by leaving the relationship.

How does commitment manifest itself in methods used to maintain relationships?

Rusbult et al. (2011) suggest that highly committed people are likely to act in ways that help to maintain the relationship, rather than add to the pressure to destroy it. This is shown clearly in situations when the partner behaves in ways that are potentially destructive, such as making nasty remarks or failing to keep their promises. In these situations, the committed person is likely to avoid the desire to retaliate and instead react positively by focusing on the positive aspects of the relationship. They are also likely to set their own preferences aside to allow for what their partner wants and also to show forgiveness for any of their partner's indiscretions. In general, the committed partner will do all that they can to see the relationship and their partner in a positive light, even if that is unrealistic and could result, at a simple level, in them putting other people's relationships down and ignoring or forgiving their partner's bad behaviour. At a more disturbing level, this might involve (as explained below) staying in an abusive relationship, as a person can feel so committed to a relationship that they convince themselves that it's not too bad, fearing that the alternative would be worse and being afraid of losing their house, children and everything else they have put into the relationship.

Think!

If you were in a relationship that you had a put a lot of time into and your partner did/said something that you didn't like, would you immediately give up on it? What would you do to try to make things better?

Do you think any of the relationship maintenance methods outlined above would be useful?

Would it make a difference if you hadn't put a lot of time and effort into the relationship?

Mini plenary

Write a paragraph of no more than 150 words to summarise the investment model. You must include the terms, *commitment*, *satisfaction*, *comparison with alternatives* and *investment size* within your paragraph.

AO2 (Application of knowledge): How does this apply in practice

Interleave me now

Socially sensitive research and relationships

There are four aspects of the scientific research process that raise ethical implications in socially sensitive research according to Sieber and Stanley (1988):

- **The research question**: Asking questions such as 'What makes victims of domestic violence return to their partners?' may be damaging to members of a particular group.
- **The methodology used**: The right to confidentiality and anonymity, for example.
- **The institutional context**: Why is an organisation funding the research?
- **Interpretation and application of findings**: How the findings might be used.

These are important considerations for anyone conducting research into how investment in a relationship might cause a person to stick with it in spite of the abuse they are suffering.

The investment model has been applied to our understanding of abuse and intimate partner violence by a number of researchers, e.g. Rusbult and Martz (1995) studied a group of women staying in a domestic violence shelter in order to understand their reasons for remaining in an abusive relationship. They found that the very factors Rusbult et al. (2011) had identified were highly significant in this decision. Women who felt a higher level of commitment were those who had less dissatisfaction (e.g. abuse wasn't too bad); had fewer alternatives (e.g. less education); and had higher levels of investment (e.g. had children with their abusive partner). In these cases the women were more likely to stay with or return to the relationship.

Think!

What is it about this research that is socially sensitive?

Are there clues here to why this might cause problems for other groups of women in this situation?

The socially sensitive nature of this kind of research might push some to believe that this form of research should be avoided. Indeed Downes et al. (2014) have argued that such considerations have made ethical clearing for such research more challenging, which in turn has led to a dangerous lack of evidence about this issue. However, it could be that we still have a duty to carry on with such research in spite of the ethical implications, as long as we encourage due diligence in the planning of such work.

Question time

Should research into how investment affects abusive relationships be conducted?

Does it do more harm than good or is it useful?

If we find that investment and commitment are important in these situations, is there anything that could be done to help?

Mini plenary

Mandy has been married to Nick for 20 years and in that time, she can't remember being particularly happy for more than a few moments at a time. Nick has had a number of affairs, including one with their four children's babysitter. Nick spends a lot of time at the pub, and when he gets drunk he can be quite verbally abusive to Mandy, although he's never been physically abusive. Mandy's friends all tell her that she should leave him, but she's not sure where she would go – and after all Nick's not that bad!

What would Rusbult's investment model say about the reasons for Mandy staying with Nick?

AO3 (Analysis and evaluation of knowledge): How useful is this explanation?

Does investment have support from a range of studies?

One of the problems with psychological theories is that there is often contradictory evidence, so one study provides evidence in favour while another one goes against. Consequently, a good source of evidence can come from a meta-analysis, as this takes evidence from a range of studies and helps to provide a good bank of evidence that can show if the theory has widespread support.

One such meta-analysis was conducted by Le and Agnew (2003) with a sample of nearly 50 studies covering more than 10,000 participants, all investigating some or all of the variables involved in investment theory. They found that the three main factors associated with the investment model, satisfaction, quality of alternatives and investment size, were all highly correlated with commitment, and that satisfaction was the most significant of these three. They found no significant differences between men and women on these three factors.

The fact that the data is taken from such a wide range of studies, using such a large number of participants, significantly increases the validity of the investment model as an explanation for how and why couples stay together and, as it is a model that doesn't just deal with satisfaction alone, it is applicable to a wider range of relationship types, in particular abusive relationships (studies of which were included in the sample).

However, there were some shortcomings in the study, as it included studies that weren't related to romantic relationships (they were workplace-related) and this brings the study's validity into question. In addition, most of the studies used were of white, heterosexual relationships, which therefore makes it difficult to apply to non-white, homosexual relationships, further questioning the generalisability of the model.

Is it the same for homosexual relationships?

One of the criticisms levelled at a lot of research into relationships is that it has only investigated, and so only applies to, heterosexual relationships. This creates a problem of bias and the research could be charged with ignoring a significant section of society.

However, Duffy and Rusbult (1986) decided to compare the effect of investment on both heterosexual and homosexual couples in order to find out if commitment was a major influence in both, or whether there might be some other factors involved in homosexual relationships. They used a questionnaire to measure a range of factors associated with satisfaction and commitment in both kinds of relationships.

In line with Thibaut and Kelley (1978), they found that satisfaction was associated with greater levels of benefits and lower levels of costs but, crucially, in line with the investment model, they also found that greater commitment in a relationship was associated with greater satisfaction, greater investments and poorer quality of alternatives. The main difference in these findings was that women reported that they had invested more and were more committed to their relationships than men did (within heterosexual relationships) and the levels of investment and commitment for heterosexuals was only marginally greater than for homosexuals.

This suggests that gender is more significant than sexual preference in looking at different levels of investment and commitment in a relationship and therefore there is very little difference between heterosexual and homosexual couples in relation to investment. It seems that whichever type of relationship someone is in, an analysis of costs and benefits is what makes them feel satisfied but it is commitment that will keep them in the relationship.

Is there more or less commitment in marginalised relationships?

The research above suggested that sexual preference didn't affect the relationship between commitment and couples staying together, so it seems that there is the same level of commitment. However, it could be argued that relationships for which there is a certain level of social disapproval might actually need higher levels of commitment for couples to stay together as they have greater external pressure placed on their relationship.

Lehmiller and Agnew (2006) set out to test this idea using the factors identified in the investment model, as they argued that there was plenty of research to show that couples in so-called marginalised relationships are disapproved of more than people in more mainstream relationships. They chose homosexual relationships, interracial relationships and age-gap relationships (couples with an age gap of more than ten years) as their examples of marginalised relationships.

They used the investment model scale to investigate this phenomenon and found that marginalised couples did indeed invest less into their relationships than non-marginalised couples. However, they also found that marginalised couples compensated for this by having much lower belief in the quality of alternatives. Consequently, commitment to the relationship was maintained by this factor rather than by a large investment. The researchers did not find a consistent finding concerning satisfaction for all marginalised couples, but did find that age-gap couples tended to be more satisfied than non-marginalised couples, whereas homosexual couples were less satisfied and interracial couples were about the same.

Overall, the findings suggest that there may be a certain level of reactance to the prejudice and discrimination that is sometimes aimed at marginalised couples, and that this helps to push them closer together as the alternatives come to be seen as much poorer quality.

Are there methodological problems with investment model research?

Rusbult and others have used an investment model scale to assess the factors that affect commitment in a relationship, which is a form of self-report that asks people questions about their level of satisfaction/investment/quality of alternatives.

Seemingly, this causes problems because it relies on honesty and clearly there is the potential for a social desirability bias in the responses, as participants attempt to make their relationship seem better/worse than it really is. Social desirability is a regular feature of self-report measures and poses a problem for the validity of a study as we cannot be certain that the responses reflect the true feelings of the participants.

However, it's hard to imagine how else information about how satisfied someone is with their relationship could be gathered. What better measure is there of the feelings that someone has in their relationship than the individual themselves? It may be subjective, but such matters are inevitably subjective as there is nothing objective about someone's feelings.

Rusbult et al. (1998) tested the reliability and validity of the scale in order to find if there was good internal consistency in the measures used and to see if the variables measured by the scale were associated with other variables used to measure relationship satisfaction, e.g. level of trust. They were able to show that the measures had both reliability and validity in relation to these issues, and as such they argued that the scale is a very useful instrument for assessing commitment in relationships, providing results from which valid conclusions can be drawn about the effect of commitment.

This means that even though it could be argued that there is a problem of validity with using self-reports in this way, it's hard to imagine a better way of doing it. Besides which, Rusbult et al. have tested the scale and found it to be both reliable and valid.

Question time

Is there likely to be a social desirability bias in the use of the investment model scale? If so, how?

How else could the three factors of satisfaction/quality of alternatives/investment be measured?

Is there a better way to study it?

Mini plenary

Using the evaluation points for the three theories of romantic relationships looked at so far, compare the strengths and weaknesses of them in the table below.

	Social exchange theory	Equity theory	Rusbult's investment model
Strengths			
Weaknesses			

According to the investment model, commitment is at the heart of a good relationship and that commitment is a much greater predictor of a long-lasting relationship than satisfaction. However, this doesn't necessarily mean that the relationship will be happy or even any good.

New research

WKND

Are you over-committed?

Oksana Tashakova

17 October 2014

The author of the article argues that while most of the time commitment in a relationship can be regarded as a good thing, it is possible to have over-commitment. It has been suggested that over-commitment can make people defensive and negative and in the long run cause problems with self-esteem and actually put the relationship in danger. The problem is caused by relationship-contingent self-esteem (RCSE).

RCSE has been investigated at the University of Houston by Chip Knee and his colleagues (2008), who carried out a number of studies to understand this phenomenon better. They suggest that, when someone invests a lot into a relationship, they can start to measure their own feeling of self-worth against their perception of how the relationship is going, consequently minor disagreements come to be seen as major problems and people can become obsessive and needy with regard to love and romance.

The people suffering with this condition tend to feel badly about themselves as these things are happening in spite of all of their commitment and investment. This leads to negative feelings about the whole of the relationship and can lead to problems with the health of the relationship as well as mental health problems for the individuals involved.

Question time

What does this suggest about commitment as a factor in romantic relationships?
Does this tell us anything about abusive relationships?

What other factors are important in relationships?

What should partners do to avoid over-commitment?

1. What is meant by investment in romantic relationships?
2. What is the difference between interdependence and dependence in relationships?
3. What are the three factors that combine to create commitment in relationships?
4. How does commitment manifest itself in methods used to maintain relationships?
5. What is socially sensitive research?
6. What are the ethical issues involved in research into abusive relationships?
7. Should research into domestic violence be carried out?
8. Is there support for the investment model from a range of studies?
9. Is the need for investment the same for homosexual relationships?
10. Is there more or less commitment required in marginalised relationships?
11. Are there methodological problems with research into the investment model?
12. Can you be over-committed to a relationship?
13. Does this help to understand abusive relationships?

Glossary

Key word	Definition
Anonymity	The right to not have your identity revealed when giving information.
Commitment	Feeling dedicated to something and unlikely to give up easily.
Comparison with alternatives	The idea that people are satisfied in their relationships based on the extent to which they perceive their ability to exchange their current relationship for a better one.
Confidentiality	The right to have information kept private so that no one else gets to know about it.
Costs and benefits	A comparison of how much you have put in and how much you get out of a relationship.
Dependence	The extent to which an individual 'needs' a given relationship or relies uniquely on that particular relationship for attaining desired outcomes.
Ethical implications	The possible impact of psychological research on individuals or groups in society.
Extrinsic investments	Resources that arise out of the time and effort put into the relationship, such as children or a house.

Key word	Definition
Interdependence	Focuses on two people providing benefits for one another, which help them achieve a goal, even if they aren't considered equal value.
Interracial relationships	Relationships in which each partner is from a different ethnic group.
Intimate partner violence	Violence carried out by your partner in a relationship, also known as domestic violence.
Intrinsic investments	Resources that are closely tied to the relationship, such as time and emotional effort.
Investment model	A theory of relationships that suggests that level of commitment is important in understanding why people stay in a relationship.
Investment size	How much you have put into a relationship.
Marginalised relationships	Relationships that tend to bring social disapproval from others in society.
Meta-analysis	A method of research using data from a number of previous studies to try to establish an overall trend.
Reactance	Occurs when a person feels that someone is taking away or limiting their choices, so they deliberately go against the limitations set.
Satisfaction	Feeling that your relationship is healthy and going well.
Social desirability bias	The tendency to respond to questions in a way that you think will be viewed more favourably by others.
Socially sensitive research	Psychological research that can affect not only the individuals involved in the research but also other individuals and groups in society.

Plenary: Exam-style questions and answers with advisory comments

Question 1.

Explain what is meant by the term investment in relation to romantic relationships? [2 marks]

Marks for this question: AO1 = 2

Advice: In a question like this, it's important to make sure you are making it clear how this relates to psychology, so this will probably require an example. There is no need to provide any analysis or evaluation as both marks are for AO1: Knowledge and understanding.

Possible answer: Investment in romantic relationships refers to how much each partner has put into the relationship. Investments can be intrinsic and strongly tied to what you put into a relationship, e.g. time and effort, but also extrinsic, arising out of the relationship e.g. children and a house. The size of the investment is important because the more that has been put in, the more a person becomes committed and the more they have to lose if the relationship ends.

Question 2.

Describe and evaluate Rusbult's investment model of romantic relationships. [16 marks]

Marks for this question: AO1 = 6 and AO3 = 10

Advice: This question is looking for both skills of knowledge and understanding and analysis and evaluation. As there are 6 marks for AO1 and 10 for AO3, there should be greater emphasis on the evaluation. However, all such extended writing questions are marked holistically and therefore it is important that the knowledge is accurate and detailed and that the evaluation is clear and effective.

Possible answer: Rusbult's investment model is an explanation for why couples stay together in relationships and is based around the idea that investment increases a person's commitment to a relationship and makes them more likely to stick with it. The theory has developed out of interdependence models of relationships but the focus here is more on dependence and how people come to feel like they need the relationship in order to achieve the outcomes they desire.

Commitment is the most important part of the theory and is made up of three factors that come together to make the person feel tied to the relationship. Satisfaction is the first factor and is judged on the basis of costs and benefits such that if the costs of a relationship are low and the benefits are high then the relationship is likely to be satisfying. The second factor is comparison with alternatives and is based around an analysis of what else is available to a person outside the relationship. If a person looks around and believes that the potential alternatives are of poor quality, then they are more likely to stick with their current relationship. Last, but by no means least, is investment size, which refers to how much a person has put into the relationship. Investments can be intrinsic and directly related to the relationship, such as time and effort, but they can also be extrinsic, as they arise out of the relationship, such as a house and children. A high level of investment is likely to encourage a person to stay with their current relationship.

These three factors combine to create a high level of commitment to a relationship so that a person who feels a high degree of satisfaction, has low quality alternatives and has put a lot of investment into the relationship is likely to feel committed and stay. Committed partners work hard to make sure that their relationship continues in spite of the behaviour of their partner. At a simple level, this might involve putting other people's relationships down and ignoring or forgiving their partners bad behaviour. At a more disturbing level, this might involve staying in an abusive relationship, as a person can feel so committed to a relationship that they convince themselves that it's not too bad, fearing that the alternative would be worse and being afraid of losing their house, children and everything else they have put into the relationship.

The application of this theory to abusive relationships is somewhat socially sensitive as it appears to provide a reason for why people (usually women) stay in relationships where they have experienced intimate partner violence. This could have ethical implications as it might be seen as almost encouraging women to stay in such situations as there seems to be a rational basis, whereas most people would see it as completely irrational. However, Sieber and Stanley have argued that researchers should not hold back from this research as it does provide us with a better understanding, which will hopefully show how we can do something about it in the future.

There has been a wealth of research into this model and Le and Agnew conducted a meta-analysis of nearly 50 studies into the effect of commitment on relationships and found that all three of the factors identified above increased the level of commitment felt by people in relationships. They also found that satisfaction was the most significant of the three factors in explaining commitment and that this was equally true for men and women. Due to the range of research covered by this analysis and the sheer number of participants involved, over 10,000, there seems to be a high level of validity in this model. However, one issue with this research is that most of the studies were of white, heterosexual relationships.

The question of the applicability of the model to homosexual relationships was investigated by Duffy and Rusbult who found that there was no significant difference between heterosexual and homosexual relationships in this regard and that commitment was the most important factor in determining relationship endurance in both types. In fact, they found that gender was a more significant difference than sexual preference and that women were more committed to the relationship as they had invested more than men.

It has sometimes been assumed that people in marginalised relationships, which are those that experience a level of social disapproval, such as homosexual, interracial and those with a large age gap, might be more committed due to the prejudice and discrimination that they are subjected to. However, research into this area by Lehmiller and Agnew found that there was actually less investment into these types of relationships but that commitment was maintained by a comparison with alternatives that suggested that the alternatives were of poorer quality, and this helped to maintain the current relationship.

One of the potential problems with all of this research is that it is generally based on self-reports from the people involved in the relationship, which could suggest a level of social desirability bias as people might feel the need to say something that they believe the researcher will approve of. Unfortunately, it's probably impossible to do this research in any other way as it is dealing with subjective feelings for which there is no real objective measure and besides it's hard to imagine who would know more about the relationship than the partners themselves. Furthermore, the reliability and validity of the investment model scale that has regularly been used to test commitment was checked by Rusbult et al. who found it to have a high level of internal consistency and to be associated strongly with other measures of relationship satisfaction, e.g. level of trust. Consequently, it seems as though it is a measure from which valid conclusions can be drawn.

References

Downes, J., Kelly, L. and Westmarland, N. (2014) Ethics in violence and abuse research – A positive empowerment approach. *Sociological Research Online*, 19 (1): 1–13.

Duffy, S.M. and Rusbult, C.E. (1986) Satisfaction and commitment in homosexual and heterosexual relationships. *Journal of Homosexuality*, 12 (2): 1–23.

Le, B. and Agnew, C.R. (2003) Commitment and its theorized determinants: A meta-analysis of the investment model. *Personal Relationships*, 10 (1): 37–57.

Lehmiller, J.J. and Agnew, C.R. (2006) Marginalized relationships: The impact of social disapproval on romantic relationship commitment. *Personality and Social Psychology Bulletin*, 32 (1): 40–51.

Rusbult, C.E. (1980) Commitment and satisfaction in romantic associations: A test of the investment model. *Journal of Experimental Social Psychology*, 16 (2): 172–186.

Rusbult, C.E. and Martz, J.M. (1995) Remaining in an abusive relationship: An investment model analysis of non-voluntary dependence. *Personality and Social Psychology Bulletin*, 21 (6): 558–571.

Rusbult, C.E., Agnew, C. and Arriaga, X. (2011) The investment model of commitment processes. In: P.A.M. Van Lange, A.W. Kruglanski and E.T. Higgins (eds), *Handbook of Theories of Social Psychology*, Vol. 2. London and Thousand Oaks, CA: Sage, p. 218.

Rusbult, C.E., Martz, J.M. and Agnew, C.R. (1998) The investment model scale: Measuring commitment level, satisfaction level, quality of alternatives, and investment size. *Personal Relationships*, 5 (4): 357–387.

Sieber, J.E. and Stanley, B. (1988) Ethical and professional dimensions of socially sensitive research. *American Psychologist*, 43 (1): 49.

Tashakova, O. (2014) Are you over-committed? *WKND*, 17 October.

Chapter 9
Theories of romantic relationships 4: Duck's phase model of relationship breakdown

AO1 (Knowledge and understanding): Theories of romantic relationships: Duck's phase model of relationship breakdown

The process of relationship breakdown

When you're asking how relationships break down, you're not necessarily asking what causes them to break down but rather what happens when a relationship is coming to an end? Does it all happen in one great dramatic collapse or is it more of a slow drawn-out process with distinct phases that are common to the ending of all relationships? This was the issue addressed by Duck's phase model of relationship breakdown.

The phases of relationship breakdown

According to Duck (1982), relationships continue until they reach a turning point that marks the end of normal relations and a shift to a new form, which Duck refers to as the threshold, beyond which the relationship starts along a different path. This threshold can be seen from the changing perspective of one partner towards the relationship that is brought about by a feeling of dissatisfaction with how things are going.

Intrapsychic phase

The relationship begins to break down once one partner has reached the threshold of '*I can't stand this any more*', which then leads on to a cognitive process that involves the personal thoughts they are having about the relationship. It's likely that they have been going over this in their head for a while and this continues now, although they may decide to share their feelings with a close friend. They start to think about the costs and benefits of staying in the relationship and consider the alternatives to decide whether it would be the right thing to do, and if they should share their thoughts with their partner.

Dyadic phase

Once the dissatisfied partner has thought it all through, they may reach the threshold of '*I would be justified in withdrawing*', which leads on to an interactional process in which the dissatisfied partner will confront their partner with their thoughts and feelings. This will involve a discussion about who did what and whether the relationship can be saved. It's possible at this phase that the relationship could be repaired if one or both were prepared to change their behaviour; however, if not, then the relationship is likely to move on to the next phase.

Social phase

The failure of the interactions between the partners may lead to another threshold being reached '*I mean it*', which now involves the wider social networks of each partner. The dissatisfied partner will decide to go public with their concerns and start telling people that the relationship has broken down and give their reasons why. This will lead to a period of encampment as their friends start to take sides, which will lead to further discussions about the rights and wrongs of each partner. But, effectively, this is the end of the relationship as the point of no return has been reached. Some will still attempt to reconcile the couple, but the fact that it's public and so many have apportioned blame means that it will be hard for either partner to go back.

Grave-dressing phase

Once the threshold of '*It's now inevitable*' has been reached and the relationship is over, it's time to prepare for the funeral and also a time to reflect on what happened and how the relationship will now be presented to the outside world. This is likely to involve a period in which each partner tries to get over what has happened by creating both a public and private face, which are not necessarily the same. They will want to ensure that they are seen positively by everyone else and ensure that no blame can be placed on them, and they will also need to protect their own self-esteem, so the public face will be focused on blaming the partner.

The private version is more likely to focus on why the partner wasn't right in the first place and therefore concludes that there was nothing that could have been done. This will then help the person move on to the next relationship safe in the knowledge that they are a good person and that all they have to do is find the right partner and it will all be OK.

In the new version of the model, Rollie and Duck (2006) add a final phase that occurs once the person has decided it's 'Time to get a new life', which involves resurrection phase that occur as people feel the need to revert to the norm of having a partner. In order to ensure that the same mistakes aren't made next time, they may try to avoid certain types that are associated with their previous relationship, e.g. no more teachers for me! This will help them move forward positively, safe in the knowledge that nothing like that will happen again as they will find Mr/Ms Right this time.

Think!

Does this sound like the way relationships come to an end or do you think it's likely to be more dramatic than this?

Is it possible for both partners to go through these phases or is it just the one that becomes dissatisfied first?

Is it always necessary to have at least one person to blame in these situations?

Mini plenary

Draw a line to connect each correct definition with the appropriate term.

Term	Definition
Grave dressing phase	Looking for a new partner but trying to make sure that the same mistakes aren't made in a new relationship.
Intrapsychic phase	Trying to make sure that you are seen positively by everyone once the relationship is definitely over.
Resurrection phase	The time to open up to your partner about how you feel, which will either end the relationship or repair it.
Dyadic phase	A time to think about the costs and benefits of the relationship, having reached a feeling that it can't stay the same as before.

AO2 (Application of knowledge): How does this apply in practice?

Interleave me now

Idiographic vs nomothetic and Duck's phase model

The idiographic approach suggests that we should recognise the uniqueness of all individuals and focus on the specific rather than the general. This involves attempting to study individual cases in order to provide a fuller and more in-depth explanation.

The nomothetic approach, on the other hand, tries to create general laws or rules to be able to explain human behaviour, so that we can predict future behaviour and potentially control it or at least accommodate it in some way.

Question time

Which of these two approaches is more relevant to Duck's phase model?

Why is it useful to be able to explain the formation and development of relationships in this way?

Would it be better or worse to use a different approach?

Mini plenary

Ginger is in an unhappy relationship and has been thinking for some time about what to do. She has finally decided that enough is enough; she has decided to tell Fred how she feels and to talk through her reasons with him, as she feels that she has good reasons for wanting to split. Once Ginger has told Fred how she feels, she intends to change her Facebook status to single, as she wants everyone to know that she is the one who wants to end it. She thinks that will also be a good time to start tidying up her page so that the old photos of them together are no longer there and she can put up some new ones showing how happy she is now.

Identify the phases of Duck's model from the material provided above and explain why that section fits with the model.

AO3 (Analysis and evaluation of knowledge): How useful is this explanation?

Does the model explain or just describe relationship breakdown?

One of the main criticisms aimed at the model is that it fails to provide an explanation of relationship breakdown, it just describes what happens. This is a problem because we are not getting a full picture of relationship dissolution, just an idea of the likely stages that are gone through until people finally give up and go their separate ways.

Other stage/phase explanations do try to provide this kind of explanation. For example, Kayser and Rao (2006) provide an alternative phase model of relationship breakdown that follows a very similar pattern to that of Duck. Kayser and Rao's model has phases that go from the point at which disappointment with the relationship starts to emerge (sometimes before the ink is dry on the marriage certificate) through to increasing anger and ending with apathy and indifference. However, what they also do is explain where the disappointment that almost inevitably leads to the end of the relationship comes from; according to them, it's due to people going through the early stages of relationships with rose-coloured glasses. In the early stages of relationships, they argue, people have a tendency to ignore the things they don't like about their partner based on the belief that it will all be okay when they get married. Unfortunately, when they do get married, they are wearing new, clear glasses and the problems that they were prepared to ignore before are now extremely irritating and can cause immediate problems. So, this model provides more than just a description of the process, it actually explains where those problems may come from.

However, it should be considered that Duck's model wasn't really intended to provide an explanation, so it's not really fair to criticise it for not doing something that it didn't really claim to do in the first place. That would be like blaming a football commentator for doing nothing more than describing what is happening on the pitch – when that is all they've been asked to do.

Is the model complete?

Duck's model was introduced back in 1982 and since then there have been many new attempts to explain the process of relationship breakdown that have taken sometimes a slightly different and sometimes a very different approach. In 2006, Rollie and Duck attempted to amend the original Duck model because they felt that something was missing. Duck himself argued that the model was faulty because it failed to take account of the very important role of communication in the break-down process (Duck, 2005).

Consequently, Rollie and Duck made amendments to the model that reinforced the role of communication while still keeping the same basic structure of the phase model itself. In the new model, communication was emphasised at every phase. For example, in the intrapsychic phase what became more important was the lack of communication and social withdrawal on the part of the dissatisfied partner, which would be easy to spot as they became more self-focused and boring. In the dyadic phase the communication becomes limited to the couple as they withdraw from communication with others to hash things out together. Apart from this increased focus on communication, Rollie and Duck also add an extra phase to the process, which occurs after grave-dressing. This is referred to as a resurrection phase, which refers to the resurrection of the person's romantic life as they attempt to move on and find a new partner. As was said earlier, the person will try to avoid making the same mistakes by providing themselves with a list of 'things to avoid' in the future, like no more extroverts or no more blondes!

Rollie and Duck argue that the new model makes up for the problems with the old one and relates more closely to real life by focusing on both communication and the importance that the person's social network plays in the process of dissolution.

Has Facebook changed the process of relationship dissolution forever?

Duck regards social networks as really important in the process of relationship breakdown, and by this he meant all of the people that the person is going to come into contact with. However, the advent of social media has changed our understanding of social networks, as this has become a much wider group than simply the people we would have come into contact with on a day-to-day basis in the past. In the modern world, social networks are all of those people who have access to our Facebook or Twitter account.

This changing face of social networks may have changed how relationships start and break down for good, leaving Duck's model as something that should be confined to history. However, in the research of Lefebvre et al. (2015), they found that the process of relationship breakdown with users of Facebook follows very similar phases to those set out in Duck's model, just not necessarily in the same order. The research showed that the emphasis on the communication processes set out in the later Rollie and Duck model was largely mirrored in the actions of Facebook users. In the sample of 226 Facebook users they questioned, those users would withdraw from Facebook activity in the intrapsychic phase, use changes in their relationship status to go public in the social phase (earlier than suggested by the model), use surveillance strategies during the dyadic phase to keep an eye on the behaviour of their former partner and remove pictures and contacts during the grave-dressing phase.

This suggests that the model applies well to the modern world of social networking, even if the order isn't exactly the same, but Lefebvre et al. did comment that there were some differences in that being on Facebook made it difficult for the partners to make a clean break and they often remained in some kind of contact over Facebook for some time after the break-up.

Are there cultural differences in relationship breakdown?

It is often suggested that there are significant cultural differences in relationship breakdown. Specifically Moghaddam et al. (1993) have argued that the difference is between individualistic and collectivistic cultures, in that people in individualistic couples may well go through the phases identified by Duck. On the other hand, those in collectivistic cultures are subjected to significant family or social pressures that means the breakdown is entirely different as couples have less freedom to simply decide to separate.

However, Afifi et al. (2013) looked into the process of divorce from a cultural and social network viewpoint with Mexican Americans and argued that the issue wasn't as simple as the difference between individualistic and collectivistic cultures but was more closely tied to the kind of social networks that couples found themselves in and that there were individual differences based on this. Nonetheless, they did find that families played a large part in the process and that, in the communities they studied, divorce was regarded as a whole family matter, not just one for the couples themselves. Therefore divorce was 'our divorce' for the family, not just for the couple.

Consequently, the decisions over who did what and how couples should act during the process wasn't just one decided by the couple but by both families and, unlike the white American approach, which was to have two separate families after the divorce, all of those involved would still be part of one family after the divorce, as their social networks, rather like the Facebook users, would keep them in regular contact with one another.

However, it is worth noting that the study was only done with married couples and only with those with children, so it's not representative of all couples in this situation.

Question time

Does the evidence above suggest that Duck's model explains the process of relationship breakdown?

What other factors are not considered in this model?

Mini plenary

Using the evaluation points for Duck's phase model, consider the arguments for and against Duck's model as an explanation of the process of relationship breakdown.

Arguments for	Arguments against

A modern issue – practical applications for counselling and mediation

Duck's model may have useful practical applications, particularly in relation to the role of couples counselling or mediation as communication seems to be the most important part of the model.

New research

PSYCHOLOGY TODAY

10 steps to effective couple's communication

Suzanne Degges-White

3 May 2016

The author of the article suggests 10 ways of making communication more effective between couples.

1. Get comfortable – and if it's a difficult topic you plan to discuss, finding some place relatively 'neutral' works best. Don't talk about money in bed, for instance.
2. Give your partner your full **attention**. Turn off or put down any distracting technology. Lean in towards your partner a little bit.
3. Look at your partner and make eye contact. Don't try and 'stare down' your partner, but don't send a message that you're afraid to face your partner, either.
4. Open up with an 'I statement' that takes the pressure off your partner.
5. Invite your partner to share their perceptions that use an open question (one that doesn't invite a one- or two-word answer).
6. Don't interrupt! Stay focused, attentive, and connected. Even if you particularly like or simply don't agree with what is being said. Hang in there and keep your focus on the overarching goal of honest communication – a better relationship.
7. Reflect back to your partner what you think your partner is saying – check in with your partner to make sure you are hearing the overall message, not just the words.
8. Use collaborative language and recognise that when the two of you are in a room, there's a third entity present – the relationship.
9. If there's a problem that you are trying to solve, communicate your ideas for solutions with tentativeness. Maybe something like, 'Well, perhaps we could try …'.
10. Keep the communication flowing, be willing to listen, make sure you are really hearing the message your partner is sending, and don't be afraid to say you don't know.

Question time

What does this suggest about the importance of communication in romantic relationships?

Could this help couples to stay together? At what stage of Duck's model could it be helpful?

Could this help couples even if they're not going to stay together?

1. What does Duck's phase model try to explain?
2. What is the intrapsychic phase of relationship breakdown?
3. What is the dyadic phase of relationship breakdown?
4. What is the social phase of relationship breakdown?
5. What is the grave-dressing phase of relationship breakdown?
6. What is the resurrection phase?
7. What's the difference between an idiographic and nomothetic approach?
8. Is Duck's model idiographic or nomothetic?
9. Would the other approach be better or worse for understanding relationship breakdown?
10. Does the model explain or just describe relationship breakdown?
11. Is the model complete or does it need more?
12. Has Facebook changed the process of relationship breakdown forever?
13. Are there cultural differences in relationship breakdown?
14. How can communication help with a relationship that is breaking down?

Glossary

Key word	Definition
Couples counselling	A type of therapy for people in a relationship to try to resolve their problems.
Duck's phase model	A descriptive representation of the stages that relationships go through when they are breaking down.
Dyadic phase	The second stage of relationship breakdown, which involves the dissatisfied partner sharing their feelings with their partner.
Grave-dressing phase	The final phase of relationship breakdown, which involves the dissatisfied partner tidying up what's left of their relationship to make it clear that it's all over.
Idiographic approach	An approach to the study of human behaviour that is individualistic and tries to provide a more detailed understanding of single cases.
Interactional process	Discussions that take place over a period of time between the partners in a relationship.
Intrapsychic phase	The first stage of relationship breakdown, which involves the dissatisfied partner deciding that enough is enough.

Key word	Definition
Mediation	A form of dispute resolution used as an alternative to legal mechanisms, which usually happens after a divorce or relationship breakdown.
Mexican Americans	People of Mexican origin who now have American citizenship.
Nomothetic approach	An approach to the study of human behaviour that uses methods that allow for generalisation and the creation of general laws.
Relationship dissolution	The process of breaking up romantic relationships.
Resurrection phase	Once the relationship is over, a person will start to prepare for their new life.
Rose-coloured glasses	Seeing everything in a positive and optimistic manner.
Social network	All the people who are in the group of people that an individual is in contact with.
Social phase	The third phase of relationship breakdown, which involves the dissatisfied partner going public with their feelings about the relationship.
Threshold	The point at which something becomes intense enough to produce an effect.

Plenary: Exam-style questions and answers with advisory comments

Question 1.

Outline the dyadic phase of Duck's phase model of relationship breakdown? [2 marks]

Marks for this question: AO1 = 2

Advice: In a question like this, it's important to make sure you are making it clear how this relates to psychology, so this will probably require an example. There is no need to provide any analysis or evaluation as both marks are for AO1: Knowledge and understanding.

Possible answer: The dyadic phase is the second stage of Duck's model and involves the dissatisfied partner deciding to share their feelings about the relationship with their partner. It happens when they reach the threshold of feeling that they are justified in ending the relationship. They will want to start a discussion about the relationship, starting with something like 'I think it's time we split up, what do you think?'

Question 2.

Describe and evaluate Duck's phase model of relationship breakdown.

[16 marks]

Marks for this question: AO1 = 6 and AO3 = 10

Advice: This question is looking for both skills of knowledge and understanding and analysis and evaluation. As there are 6 marks for AO1 and 10 for AO3, there should be greater emphasis on the evaluation. However, all such extended writing questions are marked holistically and therefore it is important that the knowledge is accurate and detailed and that the evaluation is clear and effective.

Possible answer: Duck's phase model of relationship breakdown is an attempt to explain the process that people go through when they have reached the point in the relationship when they say to themselves 'I can't stand it any more'. Duck refers to this as the threshold, which is the point at which something becomes so intense that it has an effect and, in this case, causes a change in the relationship.

The phases described by Duck are essentially stages and it's described as a model as it is meant to provide a descriptive representation of the process that relationships go through when they are breaking down. The first phase is called the intrapsychic phase and the threshold identified above will have been reached as the person will have been thinking for some time about the relationship. This is a cognitive process so it will have just involved their own thoughts, which they are unlikely to share with anyone apart from maybe a close friend.

The second phase is the dyadic phase and involves the dissatisfied partner deciding to share their feelings with their partner and start an interaction with them so that they can discuss what each person thinks they should do and share their reasons for wanting to end the relationship. This will occur once the person has reached the threshold of 'I would be justified in withdrawing'. The discussion might lead to both partners deciding to try again but it might lead to the opposite and them deciding that it can't be saved.

Following on from this, the third phase is the social phase and involves the person deciding to go public with their decision and share this with their wider social network so that they can show that 'they mean it'. Once they have gone past this threshold, they are unlikely to go back on their decision and are now mostly concerned with getting their side of the story out to ensure that they aren't blamed for the ending of the relationship.

The final phase is called the grave-dressing phase and this occurs once the threshold of 'It's now inevitable' has been reached and essentially occurs after the relationship has ended. This is a period of tidying up affairs after the relationship has died and making sure that, at least publicly, they are seen in a positive light by the people they know and by trying to deal privately with the break-up by providing reasons to explain what happened, such as 'it was never right' or 'we just weren't matched'. This will help the person to go forward and hopefully 'get a new life', leading to the part of the model, which was added later by Rollie and Duck called the resurrection phase. This last stage involves the person preparing for a new relationship by telling themselves that they won't make the same mistake again, e.g. no more psychology teachers for me!

One of the problems that has been identified with this model is that it doesn't really explain *why* relationships break down, it merely describes *how* they do. Other stage models have done this, e.g. Kayser and Rao's stage model came up with some different phases that relationships go through but also provided an explanation of the reason for the breakdown. Their argument is that in the early part of the relationship, partners are effectively wearing rose-coloured glasses and only seeing the positive aspects, but once the couple settle down and specifically in this case, get married, then those glasses are replaced by clear ones that allow them to see all of their partner's annoying habits and irritating characteristics. However, it hardly seems fair to make this accusation against Duck as the theory doesn't attempt to do anything more than describe the process.

As the world of relationships has changed so much since social media came on the scene, the model could be accused of being out-of-date and thus lacking temporal validity. However, Lefebvre et al. conducted research with users of Facebook to try to find out if the model did apply and found that their participants went through pretty much the same phases in their Facebook activity as Duck suggested, if not necessarily in the same order. They found that people would withdraw from activity when they were thinking over their relationship, like the intrapsychic phase, and once they had decided what to do would then go public with their decision by changing their relationship status to single. Once they had done this, they would then refer to a kind of online dyadic phase that involved keeping an eye on their partner's interactions before finally deciding to bury the relationship by deleting photos and contacts. This suggests that the model fits very well with social media activity, although Lefebvre et al. did suggest that Facebook relationships were different in that it is harder to completely break contact.

One further issue that has arisen from this model is the possibility that it doesn't relate to non-Western cultures and Moghaddam et al. have claimed that it only fits with individualistic cultures as collectivistic cultures are less individual and sometimes involve arranged marriages, which are not so easy to end. However, Afifi et al. studied Mexican Americans and found that it wasn't quite as simple as that and it was more to do with the kinds of social networks that people found themselves in, which would be similar to Duck's argument. Although they did also find that the family networks were different from those of white Americans in that the families of both partners in the Mexican American couples were still tied together even after the relationship had broken down, rather like the Facebook users, meaning it was difficult to make an absolutely clean break.

In their later model, Rollie and Duck went on to emphasise the role of communication in relationships. This is something that could be applied to couples counselling and mediation, as it has been shown that communication is really important when trying to keep couples together, as well as when trying to make sure that the relationship doesn't create conflict as it ends, particularly important when children are involved, so it seems that the model has clear applications in the real world.

References

Afifi, T.D., Davis, S., Denes, A. and Merrill, A. (2013) Analyzing divorce from cultural and network approaches. *Journal of Family Studies*, 19 (3): 240–253.

Degges-White, S. (2016) 10 steps to effective couples communication. *Psychology Today*, 3 May.

Duck, S.W. (1982) A topography of relationship disengagement and dissolution. In: S.W. Duck (ed.), *Personal relationships 4: Dissolving Personal Relationships*. London: Academic Press.

Duck, S.W. (2005). How Do you Tell Someone you're Letting Go? A New Model of Relationship Break-Up. *The Psychologist*, 18 (4): 210–213.

Kayser, K. and Rao, S.S., (2013). Process of disaffection in relationship breakdown. In Handbook of divorce and relationship dissolution (pp. 217–238). Psychology Press.

LeFebvre, L., Blackburn, K. and Brody, N. (2015). Navigating romantic relationships on Facebook: Extending the relationship dissolution model to social networking environments. *Journal of Social and Personal Relationships*, 32 (1): 78–98.

Moghaddam, F.M., Taylor, D.M. and Wright, S.C. (1993) *Social Psychology in Cross-Cultural Perspective*. New York: WH Freeman/Times Books/Henry Holt & Co.

Rollie, S.S. and Duck, S. (2006) Divorce and dissolution of romantic relationships: Stage models and their limitations. In: M.A. Fine and J.H. Harvey (eds), *Handbook of Divorce and Relationship Dissolution*. New York, London. Routledge, pp. 223–240.

Chapter 10
Virtual and parasocial relationships

Virtual relationships in social media: self-disclosure in virtual relationships; effects of absence of gating on the nature of virtual relationships

Parasocial relationship: levels of parasocial relationships; the absorption-addiction model and the attachment theory explanation

AO1 (Knowledge and understanding): Virtual and parasocial relationships

Virtual relationships in social media: The role of self-disclosure in virtual relationships. How the absence of gating affects the nature of virtual relationships

Parasocial relationships: The different levels of parasocial relationships and how these affect an individual's behaviour. An outline of the absorption-addiction model and the relationship between attachment type and parasocial relationships

Virtual relationships in social media

In previous chapters, there has been a lot of consideration of how the internet has changed relationships with various forms of computer-mediated communication (CMC) allowing people to interact in ways that were not possible before. CMC is a term that is used for a variety of forms of communication from texting to chat rooms, but in the context of relationships, psychologists are particularly interested in the use of social networking sites, such as Facebook and Twitter, and online dating sites, such as Tinder and Zoosk (to name just a couple). The focus of the first part of this chapter is to look at how this has affected the process of forming relationships, before going on to consider whether it is radically different from other ways of forming relationships.

The role of self-disclosure in virtual relationships

In Chapter 3, we considered the role of self-disclosure in the development of relationships and how revealing personal information about yourself to someone you want to form a relationship with can be a tricky prospect, as you have to consider how much to reveal and how soon. This is true of all relationships but there are added issues with virtual relationships as they are not conducted face to face (at least not at first) and we need to consider how self-disclosure is used in this unusual situation.

The hyperpersonal model

According to Walther (1996), self-disclosure is an essential part of CMC, as it is the only information you have about someone, consequently it tends to happen earlier in virtual relationships than it does in the face-to-face version. The lack of visual information can also lead to more intimate and detailed discussions about a person, leading to a much higher level of self-disclosure than would happen otherwise. Walther argues that both the sender and receiver of the information can alter the perception of what the person is like; the sender because they can be selective about what they say and only reveal positive information, the receiver because they may try to fill in the gaps in the information that is provided, leading to a potential idealisation of the sender, particularly if the initial impression is favourable. A further feature of this situation is anonymity, as this allows a person to feel free to say things about themselves without having to worry about the information being 'leaked' to people who know them, rather like the 'stranger on a train' phenomenon put forward by Rubin (1975), whereby you are likely to reveal more to the stranger as they don't know you and you're unlikely to see them again.

Reduced cues theory

An alternative view comes from Sproull and Kiesler (1986), which suggests that the reduction in social context cues provided by CMC means that there is considerably less social disclosure in this situation. The cues normally provided in face-to-face interactions, such as physical appearance, facial expressions and tone of voice, are not provided so the receiver of the message gets a lot less than they would otherwise. The end result of this is to create a level of deindividuation on the part of CMC users, as they lose their sense of personal identity, which ends up with them becoming belligerent and negative. This hardly sounds like the kind of communication that is going to encourage a high degree of self-disclosure.

How the **absence of gating** affects the nature of virtual relationships

One of the features of face-to-face communication is that it creates a situation in which people can erect metaphorical gates to prevent effective interaction. These 'gates' are things such as physical features, personality characteristics or geographical location, all of which can be barriers to relationships forming as they can prevent effective interaction from occurring – but none of these are present in CMC. This absence of gating means that users can become whoever they want and present a completely false impression of themselves if they wish. In this situation they may be free to self-disclose but what they disclose may bear very little resemblance to who they actually are, potentially backed up by some fake photos if they really want to go that far.

Think!

Do you think CMC encourages or discourages greater self-disclosure?

Does the absence of gates allow people an opportunity to express their real personality or the opportunity to lie about who they really are?

Is face-to-face communication always better than CMC?

Parasocial relationships

The different levels of parasocial relationships and how these affect an individual's behaviour

Parasocial relationships are relationships where one person feels as though they are involved with another person without the other person knowing about it. The term was first used by Horton and Wohl in 1956 to refer to a one-sided relationship that develops through a fascination with a character in the media, without the object of interest knowing anything about it. In short, these are forms of celebrity worship.

From this starting point, further research has been carried out using the 23-item celebrity attitudes scale (CAS) to measure attitudes towards a person's favourite celebrity (McCutcheon et al., 2002). From this different levels of parasocial relationships have been identified, so as to differentiate those that are fairly passive and low intensity from those that are highly active and involve high-intensity celebrity worship.

Entertainment-social level

This is the least intense level and occurs due to the ability of the person to entertain, which becomes a source of interaction between people who admire these abilities. Admirers find that they like to discuss what the celebrity has done and believe that learning more about the life of the celebrity is fun. This kind of gossip-laden activity has proved to be very fruitful for celebrity magazines, as people want to know more about the real lives of their favourite soap stars, for example.

Intense-personal level

This is a more intense level of worship and may go as far as the belief that someone is in love with the celebrity. This kind of worship goes beyond the entertainment abilities of the celebrity and involves a more obsessive fascination and introduces elements of fantasy as the admirer starts to imagine what it would be like to have a real relationship with the celebrity. This is similar to the kind of obsessions seen over the years with movie stars and pop stars such as The Beatles and more recently One Direction. Fans come to believe that they have a connection with the celebrity, even if they have never met them, and may say things like 'They are my soul mate'.

Borderline-pathological level

The use of the word pathological here is an indication of the level of intensity as the admirer is now leaving the realms of reality and becoming so immersed in the life of the celebrity that they believe that they have an actual relationship in which the celebrity cares about them too. They may say that they would die for them or possibly even that they will die if they can't be with them. This level pushes people to act in a potentially irrational manner as they may spend large amounts of money to show their devotion to their idol. It may even involve them in trying to contact the celebrity by phone or email, for example, and, in extreme cases, trying to follow them. This can potentially lead on to stalking – causing significant distress to the celebrity, as they now do know the admirer, even if they would rather not!

An outline of the absorption-addiction model

McCutcheon et al. (2002) used the *celebrity attitude scale* to investigate the attitudes of 249 individuals from a range of age groups (from 10 to 68) and a range of

Table 10.1 A selection of items taken from the CAS (McCutcheon et al., 2002)

Item No.	Please use the following scale in response to the items below .5 = Strongly agree; 4 = Agree; 3 = Uncertain or neutral; 2 = Disagree; 1 = Strongly disagree					
1	If I were to meet MFC in person, he/she would already somehow know that I am his/her biggest fan	1	2	3	4	5
2	One of the main reasons I maintain an interest in MFC is that doing so gives me a temporary escape from life's problems	1	2	3	4	5
3	MFC is practically perfect in every way	1	2	3	4	5
4	I share with MFC a special bond that cannot be described in words	1	2	3	4	5
5	To know MFC is to love him/her	1	2	3	4	5

educational backgrounds. From this data, they developed an explanation for parasocial relationships based around the feeling that the worshipper's life was lacking in something that could be provided by the celebrity. The person's own lack of success could be made up for by their association with someone who was clearly successful in their field and is perceived to be having an exciting life.

Absorption

The celebrity becomes the focus of the whole of the attention of the admirer, such that all that the admirer can think about and all that they do is devoted to the worship of the celebrity. They literally become so absorbed in the life of the celebrity that it is akin to a form of hypnosis in which all they can see and hear is that which comes from the celebrity.

Addiction

Like other forms of addiction, the worshipper is now so wound up in their desire to have the celebrity in their lives that they develop a need for it. This leads on to them developing a tolerance for behaviours that previously satisfied their needs, so that now they need stronger and stronger levels of involvement to satisfy them. Just like an addict, they need an increasingly larger fix.

Think!

Can you think of examples whereby people become addicted to a celebrity?

Does this have a negative effect on their lives?

Is there any way that it could be seen as being positive or healthy?

Mini plenary

Place the following terms under the correct heading of either virtual relationships or parasocial relationships:

Absence of gating   Borderline pathological   Absorption-addiction model

Hyperpersonal model   Celebrity attitude scale   Reduced cues theory

Virtual relationships	Parasocial relationships

AO2 (Application of knowledge): How does this apply in practice?

117

AO2 (APPLICATION OF KNOWLEDGE)

Interleave me now

Deindividuation and relationships

The term deindividuation was first used by Festinger et al. (1952) in an attempt to explain the behaviour of people in crowds: how the ability to feel anonymous and lose your sense of personal identity create the conditions for a crowd to turn into a mob. They suggest that when someone goes into a state of deindividuation, they are able to express their normally inhibited behaviours and they are drawn towards situations that allow them to express these.

Possibly the most famous example of deindividuation was studied by Zimbardo et al. (1973) in the Stanford Prison Experiment, in which Zimbardo and his colleagues were able to demonstrate what happens when you take away someone's personal identity and replace it with a new one of prisoner or guard. In this situation, they were able to show how people (particularly the guards) lost their inhibitions and behaved in ways that they previously thought would not have been possible. Becoming *disinhibited* seems to open up a new world of possibilities and allow people to do and say things without the constraints of their normal moral code.

Virtual relationships and the social identity model of deindividuation effects (SIDE)

The version of deindividuation expressed above seems to fit well with the view of reduced cues theory outlined earlier and leads to a negative outcome that is hardly likely to lead to positive relationships. However, a different view of deindividuation is provided by Lea and Spears (1992), who suggest that the traditional view cannot be so simply applied to CMC and that to do so would miss the influence of social identity and social categorisation on the building of relationships through CMC. They argue that deindividuation can actually facilitate the process of developing a relationship as being able to identify someone by seeing their face/physical appearance can build barriers, in a similar way to that suggested by 'gating' above, except this time Lea and Spears are focusing on how people identify themselves as part of a group and categorise others as part of an in-group or out-group in the way suggested by Tajfel (1978). Consequently, attraction or feelings of romantic love in this situation are not based on interpersonal factors but on the perception of someone's belonging to certain social groups or social categories. Feelings of love and attraction are determined by the extent to which someone appears to belong to the same groups as the communicator, such that belonging will lead to feelings of attraction that may not have been there in an individuated state. This leads to the conclusion that CMC might actually be preferable as a starting point compared to face-to-face communication or at least to individuated communication.

Question time

What is meant by deindividuation?

Is deindividuation likely to occur in CMC?

Does deindividuation make you more or less likely to develop an intimate relationship using CMC? What other factors are involved in this process?

Mini plenary

Dev has been using a dating website for some time and he has developed a liking for Pat. Dev is keen to take things further and meet up, but Pat wants to know more about Dev first. Dev is concerned about this and is worried about saying too much, in case it puts Pat off. Dev is considering making up some of the information in order to keep Pat interested.

Explain this scenario with reference to some of the ideas about self-disclosure from the theories/models of virtual relationships.

Interleave me now

Attachment types

Ainsworth and Bell (1970) studied the behaviour of infants in a situation where they were placed in a room with their mother and toys to play with (a *strange situation*). They tested the effect of a stranger being introduced and the mother firstly leaving the child alone with the stranger and then returning and attempting to comfort the child. They observed the behavioural responses of children in these situations and came up with three attachment types based around these responses. They also hypothesised about the characteristics of the adults that would produce such responses. Hazan and Shaver (1987) looked at the likely effect on the characteristics of the child as they grew into adulthood (shown in Table 10.2).

Table 10.2 Attachment types and the associated child and adult characteristics

Attachment type	Child characteristics	Adult characteristics
Secure	• Explores environment using mother as a safe base • Moderate separation distress • Easily comforted by mother on return	• High self-esteem • Trusting relationships • Comfortable sharing feelings

Table 10.2 continued

Attachment type	Child characteristics	Adult characteristics
Avoidant	• Avoids contact with mother • No sign of distress on separation • No difference between mother and strangers	• Problems with intimacy • Shows little emotion in relationships • Unwilling to share feelings with others
Resistant	• Stays very close to mother and wary of strangers • High levels of separation distress • Not easily comforted by mother on return	• Reluctant to get close to others • Extremely upset by the ending of a relationship • Concerned that their partner doesn't love them, very jealous and clingy

The attachment theory explanation of parasocial relationships

McCutcheon et al. (2006) decided to use the absorption-addiction model to test the idea that attachment type would be related to a tendency towards obsessing about or even stalking celebrities. They used 299 students and assessed both their attachment type and their attitude towards celebrity worship and stalking. They found that attachment type was not related to an attraction towards celebrities, contrary to their hypothesis, but they did find that those with an insecure attachment were more likely to condone stalking and celebrity stalking and from this they assumed that they would be more likely to engage in such behaviours also. This seems to link well with both the description of insecure-resistant types as those who are clingy and more likely to respond badly to the ending of a relationship and of insecure-avoidant types who may avoid intimacy but may respond to the ending of a relationship with rage and a desire for retaliation.

In line with the absorption-addiction model, they also found that insecure attachment types were attracted to celebrities for the 'wrong reasons' and, as such, it was not surprising that those who were more needy would develop an obsession with celebrities, which could lead to stalking.

Question time

Why do those with insecure attachments lack trust in their relationships?

Why were those with insecure attachments more likely to condone stalking?

Does this make them more likely to become stalkers?

Tony is a big fan of One Direction and was absolutely gutted when they broke up, so much so that he was unable to go out for a week when it happened. He has considered contacting them in an effort to get them back together because he feels that, once they know how much it means to him, they will realise that they have made a terrible mistake and get back together, just for him. However, he's worried that if he speaks to them and they don't do what he asks that he may need to take more drastic measures as he knows that he couldn't live with the failure.

Explain how the levels of parasocial relationships apply to Tony's behaviour.

AO3 (Analysis and evaluation of knowledge): How useful is this explanation?

Virtual relationships evaluation

Does the internet make it easier to find a romantic partner in modern society?

In modern society, it is questionable whether face-to-face communication is preferable to CMC, particularly in the area of finding a romantic partner. How do people meet one another in modern society, do we just rely on connections that are made at work, through family or down the pub? The internet has opened up the world to potential daters, meaning that we are no longer restricted by demographic factors.

Rosenfeld and Thomas (2012), have shown how important CMC is for the development of romantic relationships when they looked at the link between having access to the internet and being in a romantic relationship. They studied 4,000 participants, some of whom had access to the internet and some of whom did not. They found that 71.8 per cent of those with access to the internet were married or in a romantic relationship, compared to 35.9 per cent of those without access to the internet.

This suggests that CMC is better than a simple reliance on face-to-face communication; and it appears as though the internet really does open up a wider range of possibilities, providing a greater chance of developing a romantic relationship.

However, this data is merely correlational and doesn't take into account the many other factors involved in the chances of having a romantic partner. Furthermore, the data tells us nothing about whether the people involved used the internet to form a relationship, consequently, there is nothing to suggest that having access to the internet was anything more than a coincidental factor in someone having a romantic relationship. One thing it could indicate is that those seeking a romantic partner are more likely to have the internet, whereas those that are not don't feel the need to, so it may be more of an indication of desire to form a relationship than the actual ability to do so.

The general finding of the research conducted for the theories outlined above is that there are no significant differences between males and females in their responsiveness to relationships formed online, and that men and women are likely to value the disclosures and intimacy that comes from these situations equally. However, some research has found gender differences and, as such, it could be argued that the theories and research associated with them could be accused of beta bias if they ignore these differences.

McKenna et al. (2002) found that women placed higher value on self-disclosure, and also rated the relationships formed online as more intimate then men, particularly when the content of these disclosures was highly emotional. It seems that men were more interested in disclosures that were related to their shared interests in activities such as sports and seemed to regard the relationships formed online as less close or intimate than those formed face-to-face.

This suggests that previous research into online relationships had not taken enough account of these differences and as such had assumed that males and females were taking as much from the high levels of disclosure without fully taking into account the content of the disclosure. On the other hand, it could be argued that the findings above reflect stereotypical differences between men and women and maybe indicates a certain level of response bias in the research, as men may have been responding in ways that they thought would be appropriate and avoiding emotional disclosures for stereotypical reasons. Consequently, the research could be accused of alpha bias in assuming that these differences are real when they are nothing more than stereotypes.

An alternative view of CMC and self-disclosure

As was discussed in Chapter 3, whether or not higher levels of self-disclosure lead to greater attraction and intimacy depends on the context in which the disclosure is made (Collins and Miller, 1994). If the reasoning behind the disclosure (attribution) is believed to be non-personal, then this will be regarded as anything but intimate and lead to lower levels of attraction.

Further research by Lee et al. (2019), showed how higher levels of self-disclosure were associated with intimacy in offline relationships but that this was not the case with online relationships, as higher levels of self-disclosure actually led to lower levels of intimacy. Similar to the finding of Collins and Miller, this seemed to be associated with the attributions given to the disclosure, in particular when it was done in a situation when the perceived number of recipients was high. This seems to suggest that disclosures made through social media are not good for developing intimate relationships and that face-to-face communication would be better (for a full description of this study refer to Chapter 3).

However, this study was completed with Facebook users only and it may be that, as this site is not dedicated to dating and people know that it often contains material that is seen by a large number of users, this is somewhat different to sites dedicated to dating, where disclosure is likely to be done in a more intimate setting and may not have this problem with attribution.

Parasocial relationships evaluation

Does celebrity worship relate to addiction and criminality?

One of the suggestions of the absorption-addiction model is that those who are involved in celebrity worship can become addicted, which leads to them developing a tolerance for behaviours related to their worship and which could, as is the case with some addicts, lead them into criminal behaviour in order to feed their need for greater and greater exposure to their chosen celebrity.

A study by Sheridan et al. (2007) examined the possible connection between celebrity worship and addiction and criminality. In a study of around 3,000 participants, using questionnaires to assess both their level of celebrity worship and their level of addiction/criminality related to this, they were able to show a moderate relationship between both factors (addiction and criminality) and celebrity worship. They found that the most common aspect of addiction/criminality was related to what they referred to as deleterious imitation, which was ascertained from questions relating to issues such as 'If my favourite celebrity endorsed a legal but possibly unsafe drug designed to make someone feel good, I would try it', and 'If I were lucky enough to meet my favourite celebrity, and he/she asked me to do something illegal as a favour, I would probably do it'.

However, Sheridan et al. argued that it is not possible to propose that high levels of celebrity worship, or high scores on particular constructs of the Celebrity Attitudes scale predict addiction and criminality as this data is only correlational and cannot show cause. They suggest that it is more appropriate to conclude that their findings support the absorption-addiction model of celebrity worship and the idea that pathological levels of celebrity worship reflect attempts to establish an identity. From this they argued that it might be true to say that rather than seeking positive role models or heroes, pathological worshippers are drawn to more entertaining, even antisocial, celebrities. The kind of imitation referred to earlier may lead them into behaviour that can have negative consequences for the worshipper.

Are there individual differences in the tendency to worship celebrities?

One of the questions raised about celebrity worship concerns the extent to which we can say that it is determined by individual characteristics related to personality or some other factor. Some research has found that there are personality differences, such that the borderline pathological level of celebrity worship is associated with the psychotic personality type, e.g. Maltby et al. (2003).

One of the more unusual findings concerning individual differences in celebrity worship comes from Huh (2012), who tested the idea that digit ratio might be associated with celebrity worship, particularly among adolescents. Huh measured the digit ratios of 45 male and 61 female participants aged 12–14 and compared this with scores from the same participants on the CAS. It was found that the digit ratios for the entire sample were positively correlated with CAS scores, however, this was somewhat distorted by the higher number of female participants, as although there was a significant positive correlation for females, this was not true for males. This showed that females with lower digit ratios were less likely to worship celebrities.

This unusual finding might be related to other factors that have been associated with digit ratio. For example, it has been shown that sex hormones are responsible for differences in digit ratio, such that females are likely to have a higher digit ratio than males, suggesting that celebrity worship may be related to female sex hormones. However, this was a relatively small sample with a small age range, so it is hard to generalise from this finding to all males and females, particularly of other age groups. However, the study only intended to look at this age group, so it's hard to criticise it for not being generalisable to others that were never intended to be studied.

Is celebrity worship just a phase?

One of the issues with the use of the CAS is that it may just be measuring an attitude at that point in time and therefore the temporal stability of the measure could be questioned, as it may be just a temporary phase that the person is going through.

Griffith et al. (2013) examined the test–retest and internal reliability of a scale used to measure celebrity worship. They used the CAS on 2 different occasions approximately 3 months apart on 248 participants (167 females and 81 males), with ages ranging from 17 to 53, drawn from 3 universities and 1 college. They found that the measures of celebrity worship remained stable over time, which suggests that not only is the temporal stability of the measure sound but that the measures used are also reliable. They also found support for the absorption-addiction model in this study as those who scored higher on the borderline pathological measure were even more likely to stick with their celebrity worship – as suggested by the model, suggesting the model has good predictive validity.

Some of the positives about this study are that the sample is fairly large, the age range is quite broad and the participants were from more than just one college, which does allow for potential generalisation. However, one of the limitations recognised by the researchers is that the period studied, just three months, was rather short to draw strong conclusions about the temporal stability of the measure – which doesn't really allow us to say for sure that celebrity worship isn't just a temporary phase and it would need research to be conducted over a much longer period to say for certain if this is the case.

Question time

Does the evidence above suggest that the absorption-addiction model is a useful explanation for parasocial relationships?

Does this suggest that celebrity worship is a bad thing for people or is it relatively innocent?

Is celebrity worship linked to stalking?

Mini plenary

Using the evaluation points for virtual relationships and parasocial relationships, compare the strengths and weaknesses of them in the table below:

	Virtual relationships	Parasocial relationships
Strengths		
Weaknesses		

A modern issue – digital deception and catfishing

On the internet, people can become whoever they want and sometimes this is done in order to trick someone who is simply there looking for love. Catfishing is the term given to people who create a fake profile on the internet with the intention of deceiving or even defrauding someone.

New research

THE CONVERSATION

Have you caught a catfish? Online dating can be deceptive

Nicole Marie Allaire

23 January 2019

According to Allaire, the internet has provided the opportunity for people to adopt a different identity, as it is fairly difficult to check if they are telling the truth. This opportunity to lie with impunity has led to a rise in the number of people using social media and dating websites to deceive potential partners.

The term 'catfishing' was used in a 2010 movie and was later expanded into an MTV reality series that explores examples of this happening and there are a lot more than people might think or like to think!

Why might someone become a catfish?

Allaire argues that some people aren't necessarily intending to hurt anyone as they are sometimes just presenting an idealised version of themselves. Others are intending to deceive their targets but only because they lack self-esteem and not for any kind of malicious reasons (the TV show has a number of examples of people struggling with their sexuality who fear bullying or violence). However, there are some who use the deception in order to get revenge on former partners, or to get some attention or to defraud others.

It seems that people have a strong desire to trust the people they are communicating with, even if sometimes it appears too good to be true. The 'halo effect' seems to play a part as if people develop a liking for someone early on, they are likely to continue with this view in spite of evidence to the contrary.

A complementary idea is that of the 'hyperpersonal connection', which suggests that people who have developed deep, emotional ties with another person may become even more trusting and be prepared to share things online that they wouldn't necessarily do in person. This hyperpersonal revealing is something that the catfish do – but they are usually not telling the truth!

Another reason is that if things appear to be going well, people may not want to mess things up by questioning the honesty of the catfish, particularly if it is helping them to feel accepted and less lonely.

Allaire offers advice to those using this form of social media to develop romantic relationships: 'beware if someone gives fishy answers, do your own background checking, searching images, phone numbers and social networks like they do on the *Catfish* show.'

This may not be the most romantic way to build a relationship, but it may prevent you from getting 'hooked-up' with a catfish – who might steal more than just your heart!

Question time

What does this suggest about the importance of disclosure in virtual relationships?

Does this mean that people shouldn't use these methods for fear of being deceived?

How can people be sure that the person they're talking to is real and honest? Should the TV show be compulsory viewing for anyone thinking of going down this line?

Chapter plenary

1. What are virtual relationships?
2. What is the role of self-disclosure in virtual relationships?
3. What is the hyperpersonal model of virtual relationships?
4. What is the reduced cues theory of virtual relationships?
5. What is meant by the term absence of gating in relation to virtual relationships?
6. What are parasocial relationships?
7. What is the entertainment-social level of parasocial relationships?
8. What is the intense-personal level of parasocial relationships?

9. What is the borderline-pathological level of parasocial relationships?
10. What is the absorption-addiction model of parasocial relationships?
11. What is meant by SIDE in relation to virtual relationships?
12. What is the relationship between attachment type and parasocial relationships?
13. Does the internet make it easier to find a romantic partner in modern society?
14. Are there gender differences in CMC?
15. What is the alternative view of CMC?
16. Does celebrity worship relate to addiction and criminality?
17. Are there individual differences in the tendency to worship celebrities?
18. Is celebrity worship just a phase?
19. Are there any lessons to be learned from catfishing?

Glossary

Key word	Definition
Absence of gating	A view of CMC that suggests that it allows you to communicate more freely as there are fewer barriers in the way.
Absorption-addiction model	An explanation for how someone develops an addiction for their favourite celebrity.
Anonymity	Keeping your identity a secret.
Attachment types	Characteristic behaviours that develop in childhood in response to a mother's response to her child.
Attribution	How we explain the causes or reasons behind behaviour.
Belligerent	Responding in a hostile or aggressive manner.
Borderline-pathological level	The highest level of intensity that can have dangerous consequences, e.g. stalking.
Catfishing	Creating a false internet profile in order to deceive or defraud others.
Celebrity attitudes scale	A questionnaire used to measure someone's level of celebrity worship.
Computer-mediated communication (CMC)	Communication that occurs through some online medium, e.g. email/social media.
Deindividuation	Losing your sense of identity.

Key word	Definition
Deleterious imitation	When behaviour that could cause harm or damage is copied.
Digit ratio	A measure of the ratios of the different lengths of your 2nd and 4th digits on your hand. A high ratio suggests that they are about the same length.
Disinhibited	Behaviour that is not held back by normal social rules.
Entertainment-social level	The lowest intensity level of celebrity worship, which is based around admiration for someone's entertainment skills.
Halo effect	Forming a positive view of someone because the first impression was favourable.
Hyperpersonal connection	A connection that has a high level of intimacy.
Hyperpersonal model	A view of CMC that suggests that more intimate details are released through this medium.
Idealisation	Developing an idea about what someone is like based on an unrealistically positive view of what they might be like.
In-group	The social group that you identify with.
Intense-personal level	A middle level of intensity that is based around feelings of love for the celebrity.
Internal reliability	A measure of the consistency of items within a test.
Out-group	The social group that you don't identify with.
Parasocial relationships	Relationships where one person feels as though they are involved with another person without the other person knowing about it, e.g. celebrity worship.
Predictive validity	Whether a score is able to predict a future measurement.
Reduced cues theory	A view of CMC that suggests that fewer intimate details are released through this medium.
Self-disclosure	A process of communication by which one person reveals information about themselves to another.
Social categorisation	How people put themselves and others into groups based on their social identity.
Social identity	The sense of who you are based on your membership of a group.

Key word	Definition
Social identity model of deindividuation effects (SIDE)	An explanation for CMC that suggests that losing your sense of identity can lead to positive as well as negative effects.
Stereotypical differences	Differences between people that are based on expectations about behaviour, rather than real differences.
Temporal stability	The consistency of a measure over time.
Test–retest reliability	A measure of the consistency of a test by conducting it twice over a period of time.
Virtual relationships	A type of relationship that develops through computer mediated communication.

Plenary: Exam-style questions and answers with advisory comments

Question 1.

Explain what is meant by self-disclosure in relation to virtual relationships. [2 marks]

Marks for this question: AO1 = 2

Advice: In a question like this, it's important to make sure you are making it clear how this relates to psychology, so this will probably require an example. There is no need to provide any analysis or evaluation as both marks are for AO1-Knowledge and understanding.

Possible answer: Self-disclosure refers to the revealing of information from one person to another in a romantic relationship. This relates to virtual relationships because there is a debate in psychology about whether people reveal more or less about themselves using computer-mediated communication. For example the reduced cues theory suggests that less is revealed but the hyperpersonal model suggests more.

Question 2.

Explain what is meant by levels of parasocial relationships. [4 marks]

Marks for this question: AO1 = 4

Advice: In a question like this, it's important to make sure you are making it clear how this relates to psychology, so this will probably require an example. There is no need to provide any analysis or evaluation as all marks are for AO1: Knowledge and understanding.

Possible answer: Parasocial relationships are relationships where one person feels as though they are involved with another person without the other person knowing about it, e.g. celebrity worship. These relationships have been shown to happen at different levels of intensity, such that someone might have a low intensity feeling due to their admiration of the entertainment-social skills of the celebrity. They can be at a more intense-personal level whereby they feel as though they love the celebrity and a borderline-pathological level, which is a kind of unhealthy obsession with the celebrity whereby they feel as though the celebrity has feelings for them too.

Question 3.

Describe and evaluate research into virtual and/or parasocial relationships. [16 marks]
Marks for this question: AO1 = 6 and AO3 = 10

Advice: This question is looking for both skills of knowledge and understanding and analysis and evaluation, but unlike a lot of the other questions looked at so far, it offers a potential choice of doing just one type of relationship or both. There is enough material to do just one type, so this might be the best option. As there are 6 marks for AO1 and 10 for AO3, there should be greater emphasis on the evaluation. However, all such extended writing questions are marked holistically and therefore it is important that the knowledge is accurate and detailed and that the evaluation is clear and effective.

Possible answer: Virtual relationships are those that are conducted through computer-mediated communication (CMC) and there is a question about whether such relationships lead to higher or lower levels of self-disclosure and intimacy when we are in the process of looking to form a romantic relationship with someone.

On the one hand, there are those who believe that CMC leads to lower levels of disclosure and intimacy such as Sproull and Kiesler's reduced cues theory, which suggests that the lack of context cues such as physical appearance, facial expressions and tone of voice that are normally present in face-to-face communication are missing from CMC. This lack of cues leads people to disclose less and fail to develop a high level of intimacy because they start to lose their sense of personal identity (deindividuation) and consequently become hostile and aggressive. This means that CMC is considerably worse than face-to-face interactions and not a good means of communicating if you are hoping to form a romantic relationship with someone.

On the other hand, there is Walther's hyperpersonal model that suggests that CMC is much better as it creates the need for a person to reveal more about themselves, as the other person has nothing to go on other than what they say. This means that the information needs to be more personal and more detailed in order to get a clear impression of what someone is like. The more detailed and personal the information is, the more likely we are to develop a higher level of intimacy. The anonymity associated with this situation also makes it easier for a person to reveal more about themselves as they feel as though this information is unlikely to cause them embarrassment, as they may never actually meet the person they are communicating with and they are also unlikely to know their friends and tell them what they have said.

Connected to this model is the notion of absence of gating, which also suggests that CMC is better because there are fewer barriers than those associated with face-to-face communication. In offline situations barriers or gates are present, as things like physical appearance can hold people back from even being given the chance to disclose information, perhaps because the other person has already decided that they aren't interested just because of the way they look or speak, etc. The problem with this is that while people may feel free to disclose information, what they say may not be entirely truthful.

Some researchers have found that CMC makes it easier to form romantic relationships by looking at the connection between having access to the internet and the likelihood of being in a romantic relationship. Rosenfield and Thomas studied 4,000 participants, some of whom had access to the internet and some of whom did not. They found that 71.8 per cent of those with internet access were married or in a romantic relationship whereas only 35.9 per cent of those without internet access were in the same situation. This seems to suggest that having the internet is beneficial to developing a romantic relationship and may indicate that it is more useful for developing close relationships than face-to-face communication. However, this is purely correlational research and can therefore merely indicate that these two factors are related but cannot show that one causes the other. It could be a mere coincidence or may be that those without internet access aren't actually looking for a relationship because, if they were, they would probably have the internet!

Further issues with this are raised when we start to look at gender differences in the use of CMC in relation to self-disclosure. Research by McKenna et al. found that women tend to value online intimate self-disclosure more than men and are able to form closer relationships online. Men on the other hand are more interested in disclosing less intimate information online, such as sporting interests, and men find that they have closer offline relationships. This suggests that theories in this area have previously ignored these gender differences and so could be accused of beta bias. However, it could be that there was a certain level of response bias in men's answers to the questions posed in this research and that men might have been going along with stereotypical ideas of what men are supposed to be interested in. Consequently, the differences identified might just be stereotypical and therefore not real, and so this research could be accused of alpha bias as it has revealed differences that don't actually exist.

One of the problems with CMC referred to earlier was the possibility that someone could appear to be disclosing a lot, due to the absence of gating, but it could just be a pack of lies. This problem has been highlighted by the idea of catfishing, which happens when someone creates a false profile with the express desire of deceiving or defrauding others.

Allaire suggests that people might become a catfish for different reasons, some might be doing it to actually defraud but others may be doing it due to a lack of self-esteem or the fear of bullying that might come if they reveal their true selves. The TV show of the same name has shown how people can be easily drawn into this situation due to the need to escape loneliness, and that they fail to challenge the catfish as they fear losing out on what appears to be an ideal relationship. Unfortunately, there is no easy way round this and the practical advice that comes from Allaire is to do a bit of checking to see if you can find information from other sources about this person through Google, etc. All of which suggests that while you can get a lot of information from people online, beware if it seems 'fishy' as it may just be too good to be true.

References

Ainsworth, M.D.S. and Bell, S.M. (1970) Attachment, exploration, and separation: Illustrated by the behavior of one-year-olds in a strange situation. *Child Development*, 41: 49–67.

Allaire, N.M. (2019) Have you caught a catfish? Online dating can be deceptive. *The Conversation*, 23 January 2019.

Collins, N.L. and Miller, L.C. (1994) Self-disclosure and liking: A meta-analytic review. *Psychological bulletin*, 116 (3): 457.

Festinger, L., Pepitone, A. and Newcomb, T., (1952). Some consequences of de-individuation in a group. *The Journal of Abnormal and Social Psychology*, 47 (2S): 382.

Griffith, J., Aruguete, M., Edman, J., Green, T. and McCutcheon, L. (2013) The temporal stability of the tendency to worship celebrities. *SAGE Open*, 3 (2): 2158244013494221.

Hazan, C. and Shaver, P. (1987) Romantic love conceptualized as an attachment process. *Journal of Personality and Social Psychology*, 52 (3): 511.

Horton, D. and Wohl, R. (1956). Mass communication and para-social interaction: Observations on intimacy at a distance. *Psychiatry*, 19: 215–229.

Huh, H. (2012) Digit ratio and celebrity worship. *Personality and Individual Differences*, 52 (3): 265–268.

Lea, M. and Spears, R. (1992) Paralanguage and social perception in computer-mediated communication. *Journal of Organizational Computing*, 2: 321–341.

Lee, J., Gillath, O. and Miller, A. (2019) Effects of self- and partner's online disclosure on relationship intimacy and satisfaction. PLOS ONE, 14 (3): e0212186.

Maltby, J., Houran, J. and McCutcheon, L.E. (2003) A clinical interpretation of attitudes and behaviors associated with celebrity worship. *The Journal of Nervous and Mental Disease*, 191 (1): 25–29.

McCutcheon, L.E., Lange, R. and Houran, J. (2002) Conceptualization and Measurement of Celebrity Worship. *British Journal of Psychology*, 93 (1): 67–87.

McCutcheon, L.E., Scott Jr, V.B., Aruguete, M.S. and Parker, J. (2006) Exploring the link between attachment and the inclination to obsess about or stalk celebrities. *North American Journal of Psychology*, 8 (2): 289–300.

McKenna, K.Y., Green, A.S. and Gleason, M.E. (2002) Relationship formation on the Internet: What's the big attraction? *Journal of Social Issues*, 58 (1): 9–31.

Rosenfeld, M.J. and Thomas, R.J. (2012) Searching for a Mate: The Rise of the Internet as a Social Intermediary. *American Sociological Review*, 77 (4): 523–547.

Rubin, Z. (1975) Disclosing oneself to a stranger: Reciprocity and its limits. *Journal of Experimental Social Psychology*, 11 (3): 233–260.

Sheridan, L., North, A., Maltby, J. and Gillett, R. (2007) Celebrity worship, addiction and criminality. *Psychology, Crime & Law*, 13 (6): 559–571.

Sproull, L. and Kiesler, S. (1986). Reducing social context cues: Electronic mail in organizational communication. *Management Science*, 32 (11): 1492–1512.

Tajfel, H. (1978). *Differentiation between Social Groups: Studies in the Social Psychology of Intergroup Relations*. London: Academic Press.

Walther, J.B. (1996). Computer-mediated communication: Impersonal, interpersonal, and hyperpersonal interaction. *Communication Research*, 23 (1): 3–43.

Zimbardo, P.G., Haney, C., Banks, W.C. and Jaffe, D. (1973) A Pirandellian prison: The mind is a formidable jailer. *New York Times Magazine*, 8, pp. 38–60.

Index

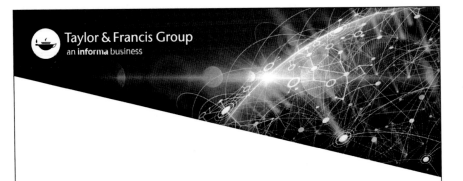